GW00391448

**Southampton's Marquis**
and other mariners

**Opposite: View of Southampton from Peartree Green.**

From a painting by David Cox (1783-1859)

# **Southampton's Marquis**
# and other mariners

A Portrait of Peartree Green
from 1740 to 1840,
wherein are the intertwined
lives of its Captains,
the 2nd Marquis of Lansdowne
and the Young Napoleon

by Gerald Mornington

**Publishing details.** First published 1984. Text copyright Gerald Mornington

**Printing credits.** Typeset by Clare Malling at the Fosse Bureau, 36 Princes Street, Yeovil, Somerset. Design by Rodney Legg. Printed in Great Britain by Wincanton Litho at the Old National School, North Street, Wincanton, Somerset, with platemaking by Andrew Johnstone and machining by Steve Taylor. Case-bound by Butler and Tanner Limited at Frome, Somerset.
**Distribution.** Trade sales distribution by Dorset Publishing Company from Knock-na-cre, Milborne Port, Sherborne, Dorset DT9 5HJ, telephone (0963) 32583. International Standard Book Number. (ISBN) 0 902129 55 4

# Contents

| | | |
|---|---|---|
| List of Illustrations | | 9 |
| Acknowledgements | | 11 |
| 1 | Peartree Green | 13 |
| 2 | The Cooksey Chronicles | 25 |
| 3 | The Family Tree | 40 |
| 4 | The 'Peartree Packets' | 48 |
| 5 | Alarums and Excursions | 59 |
| 6 | John Henry Petty, Lord Fitzmaurice | 65 |
| 7 | John Henry Petty, Earl of Wycombe | 70 |
| 8 | Wycombe's Voyages | 74 |
| 9 | A Peculiar Privateer | 86 |
| 10 | John Henry Petty, Marquis of Lansdowne | 94 |
| 11 | A Corsican on Peartree Green | 105 |
| 12 | One Last Look from Peartree Green | 114 |

# List of Illustrations


View of Southampton from Peartree Green *Frontispiece*
The Royal Oak 18
Peartree Green and Jesus Chapel 22
The Arms of St Mary Extra 28
The Duke of Richmond's cutter, *Goodwood,* a triple portrait 48
Calshot Castle, with a hoy and square-tops'l cutter outward bound 52
Itchen Ferry landing hard, with a square-tops'l cutter beached off Payne's Shipyard and at the Bryer Packet moorings a schooner resembling the type developed in the American Colonies 54
Square-tops'l cutter entering Littlehampton 57
Bowood Park, Wiltshire: the seat of the 1st Marquis of Lansdowne 66
The Earl of Wycombe with an inset of detail, the *Frisk* 79
The 'Castle' bought by the Earl of Wycombe in 1804 96
Lansdowne Castle, from the west, circa 1807 100
The new steam-driven 'Floating Bridge' at the Southampton side 116

# Acknowledgements

For material taken from previously unpublished manuscripts in public custody my acknowledgements are due to the Public Record Office (High Court of Admiralty papers concerning *Frisk* and the Wills of John Henry Petty and of his widow); the British Library (the papers of Sir Robert Murray Keith, of Henry Richard Vassall Fox, 3rd Baron Holland, and of Philip Yorke, 3rd Earl of Hardwicke, and also the rare books concerning Napoleone Buona Parte); the State Paper Office of the Republic of Ireland (confidential letter from H.F.Hill to Edward Cooke reporting Wycombe's movements, and Wycombe's request to Lord Castlereagh for a permit to leave Ireland); West Sussex County Record Office (Captain Peter Bruff's *Goodwood* accounts); Hampshire County Record Office (Land Tax returns and the Will of Josiah Bryer); and Southampton City Record Office (commercial and genealogical records).

For responding so handsomely to my request for information I am grateful to C.J.Davies esquire of Truro for establishing from newspaper reports, the official records having been destroyed, that the Marquis of Lansdowne's last yacht was the *Henry;* and to Dr J.F.A.Mason for his search among the College manuscripts for details of John Henry Petty during his time at Christ Church, Oxford, as a Noble scholar; and to T.L. Ingram esquire, FCA, Archivist of Baring Brothers and Company, for verifying the signature of John Baring (1730-1816) and for information linking John Baring with the Earl of Wycombe.

For their invaluable help in assembling the sparse and scattered published material, mostly concerning John Henry Petty, and for their correspondence on various questions of historical fact, I am grateful to Professor Anthony Bryer of Birmingham University; Vincent Cronin esquire, the Napoleonic scholar; Professor Ronald Fryer of Nottingham University; and to the Earl of Shelburne for material from the Bowood archives.

G.M.

# 1

# Peartree Green

Excepting that cricket was played upon it, as it was upon all village greens within the civilisation then spreading from Broadhalfpenny Down only a few miles away, Peartree Green was not like any other. The traveller expecting to find a square of common land bordered with orderly ranges of dwellings, a church and an inn, would be disappointed, especially when he found that the inn was a further long step away, and that down a steep bridle-path roughened and runnelled by winter's showers. This green was like a close-fitting skull-cap, covering a smooth, gently rounded, close cropped and weatherworn hilltop which was unencumbered by anything, natural or artificial, excepting a crooked tree and a wooden bench.

Unlike the houses round other greens, barefacedly glaring at one another across the void, those at Peartree, at least the taller ones, only peeped over the crest of the Green with their attic eyes; they were like ships hull-down beyond the horizon, their presence betrayed only by their topsails. The exceptions were a few houses lying at a distance to the north, beyond hedges which hid the land on which they stood, land which may have been a trifle higher than that where grew the tree and stood the bench but which then fell away. The eyes of these houses, though standing high, did not stare but only peeped because their owners had over the years been so determined to create shelter from the northerly blasts that the foliage of their oaks and elms and beeches nearly enveloped, as it appeared from the bench, the houses. Their sun-seeking windows facing across the Green looked however over miles of countryside descending to sea level with no counter-staring house intervening. These tree-girt houses owed their originally exposed positions to the presence of an abundance of cut stones in the ruins of the quays and the storehouses and the barracks which comprised the Roman station called Clausentum, together with a straight, nicely engineered road called the Ridgeway by which the stones could be taken to the very crest of the hill.

The tree that gave the Green its name was of the kind that in parts of Hampshire, and no doubt in more distant parts where Hampshire folk had taken its seed and settled, as I recently discovered in Kent, is known as a shrinkabout. Ask any old countryman, say in the New Forest, and he will reply—"That? 'Er be a li'l ol' shrinkabout." Those whose restless spirits sadly prevent them from leaving it at that, and must worrit out a professor of botany, will be told that a shrinkabout, despite the apple-like shape, colour and taste of its fruit, is a kind of wild pear. Their number is fast declining and it is rare to find two in close proximity. But for their clinging to life tenaciously, throwing out fresh shoots when bowed in extreme age and casting bushels of fruit around in the hope of regeneration, they surely would by now be extinct. Their diminutive fruits not only provide a refreshing nibble for the passing traveller but also a curious attraction to some species of butterfly. Their stature could never compare with yonder oak or elm, but in age, and some say in wisdom, the shrinkabout must be their peer. Concerning this particular shrinkabout we have the testimony of one John Duthy who visited Peartree Green somewhen between 1830 and '35. He described the general aspect of the tree as a ruin and its trunk a twisted stump and yet its branches were such that boys climbed among them. He argued that its age should be reckoned in centuries because the Green had been named from it much more than two hundred years before his visit.

The bench, at the time of which I write, was a great slab of elm, which by reason of a bad shake in its grain Mr Payne, the shipbuilder whose yard was on the shore near the Royal Oak, had rejected, was most carefully placed. It was just possible to see from it, without stirring, the whole of the outfield of the cricket pitch, the slope down to the Royal Oak, with its tables and benches shaded by a shapely tree, the curved ferry-landing nearby, the stone ferry steps at Crosshouse on the far shore, whence stretched the tree-lined promenade called the Beach above the tidewater right to the water-gate under God's House Tower in the Town's Norman walls. That way the scene embraced not only the water traffic in the Itchen but that in Southampton river which sometimes had been counted to upwards of two-hundred sail. Directly ahead, across the cricket pitch, the bench shared with the houses on the Ridgeway behind the long and broad view of which Cobbett wrote 'to them that delight in water scenes this is the prettiest place that ever I saw in my life.'

Since the mainstream of a man's philosophy is derived from the best loved and familiar scenes enjoyed by him, and since everyone in the parish had cause to cross the Green, and sometimes to rest on its bench, in the course of their daily tasks, or to attend the church, to pursue their courtship or just meet their friends, scenes which included men he knew perhaps from childhood, some nearby driving a flock or guiding the plough, others afar working their ships down to the sea, a reconstruction of the scene from and the talk that occurred at the bench might enable us to understand why one historian wrote that 'the inhabitants are said to have been always very peculiar, and chary in their dealings with natives of other parts of the country.'

Although we know from the context that this historian was referring mainly to the inhabitants of the settlement along the shore and generally called Itchen Ferry, where indeed the ferry-boats plied by right accorded to the manor of Wolston, and the fishing fleet put out and landed their catches, to be sorted, gutted and prepared for market across the river, the bench at the top of the hill was to their elders an important meeting place, a centre for the exchange of intelligence, an observation post against potential enemies even as the Roman sentries must have watched from here the approaches to Clausentum, their military station cunningly hidden round the first bend in the river. On this little island set in a sea of greensward there was no need for furtive whispering; a quite innocent-looking gathering there could safely discuss how to avoid or perhaps to fight some new hazard in its largely hostile world.

The maritime folk of St Mary Extra, the parish of which Peartree Green was the centre, had two arch and permanent enemies, the Preventative Service and the Press Gang. Customs and Excise duties had been raised and raised again and for many had reached an intolerable level, especially for those with moderate or unassured incomes whose accustomed style of living had for long included the consuption of spirits, tea and tobacco. The fishing industries everywhere now landed other and more profitable commodities than fish, and their marketing involved other than the fishwives. It was a highly organised business opposed by greatly outnumbered riders and boatmen of the Preventative Service who were however sometimes assisted by the military. *The Diary of a Country Parson, 1758-1802,* kept privately by the Rev'd James Woodforde (1740-1803), provides a ready and convincing explanation why the gentry living about Peartree Green and indeed throughout the land, as well as the fishermen, farm-hands, carters and others concerned, were careful not to remember having seen gatherings of ponies at dusk, nor having heard boats approaching a desolate stretch of shore. While he was up at New College, Oxford, he and his friends, contemplating nothing but the best, ordered their Southampton Port directly from the importers, Robinson and Hartley in that town, and in later years when he was head of a substantial Parsonage household, whose upkeep became increasingly difficult as the cost of both the essential and of the simply desirable elements in middle-class housekeeping always rose but never fell, he would include his needs in bottled table-wines in the shopping-list which periodically his man took into the nearest town. Excise duty was of course included in these transactions, but his gin, rum, brandy and tea were not bought over the counter and brought home in his trap by the open road and in daylight, or delivered by the regular carrier's wagon; they came and were paid for after dark, carried by shadowy figures directed by whispers without a trace of the open bargaining, the cheerful gossip, the colour and the throng of the market place. Nor was the business concluded with the departure into the night with no more than 'Thank 'ee' for the shilling gratuity for his trouble, or with the shooting of the bolts behind the door; each consignment had to be hidden or disguised as soon as possible lest an informer cause a visit to be made by Excise men before all was prepared to re-establish a convincing appearance of innocence.

These supplies of spirits would arrive in the same containers, miniature barrels colloquially mis-called 'tubs', which the master-smuggler took onboard at some foreign port. They had been generally adopted because their size, shape and filled weight made them most convenient for handling out of the hold, over the gunnel and into the arms of the waiting boatmen, small enough not to obstruct the oars while being rowed ashore, not too heavy to be carried up the beach to the waiting ponies whose panniers were made to accept their burden and keep it secure without further delay. Finally they could be stacked in caves or cellars or other such hiding places whatever the size or shape they happened to be. Great ingenuity was needed to conceal the tubs until their contents could be transferred to conventional bottles and the staves burnt and the hoops buried.

Woodforde ran a one-in-seven extra risk which his neighbours avoided by observing the Sabbath less meticulously. On a Saturday evening in September, 1752, a tub of rum arrived too late to conceal permanently that night. On the Sunday he wrote—'We were much agitated this evening about what I had brought me yesterday. Bad reports about the Parish'—of strangers perhaps who might be Excise men or their informers. The Sabbath over there came the entry—'Monday September 17. I got up very early this Morning and was very busy all the Morn' in very necessary business.' That his agitation that Sunday was justified is shown by an entry in the diary three weeks later—'John Buck, the Blacksmith, who was lately informed against for having a Tub of Gin found in his house that was smuggled, by two Excise Officers, was pretty easy fined.' The magistrates who let off a poor blacksmith with a light fine may not have been so inclined had the Parish Priest stood in the dock. And what would his Bishop have said? Yet, only eleven days after that reminder of the risk he was taking, the diarist wrote—'October 23. Had a Tub of Brandy and a

Tub of Rum brought this Evening. Gave one of the men who brought it one shilling.' And next day—'Very busy between 8 and 10 o'clock this Morn bottling off Brandy and Rum.'

The mental pictures of these nocturnal transactions are often left obscure by the diarist's brevity, but the entry for March 29th, 1771, must stimulate the imagination; 'Andrews the Smuggler, brought me this night about 11 o'clock a bagg of Hyson Tea 6 Pd weight. He frightened us a little by whistling under the Parlour window just as we were going to bed. I gave him some Geneva (gin) and paid him for the Tea at 10/6 per Pd . . . . £3.3.0.'

The searches made in towns and villages were an indication of the lack of success in catching the smugglers at the beginning of the system. On calm nights and in likely places about the Solent and Southampton River, revenue men would silently wait, listening, or close in with muffled oars to catch a few small-time smugglers' middle men. Their tubs, kegs and bundles were taken to the Custom House and the unlucky men appeared before the magistrates. Those convicted a second time, or if they had resisted arrest, and merited a substantial sentence were given the option of serving in the navy; those unfit or unwilling to endure such service went to prison and hard labour. The seized goods accumulated until there were enough for an auction at the Custom House. But the numbers of men caught and the quantities of goods seized were trifling compared with the numbers involved in the *ad hoc* network for transit and distribution and the quantities in untold and ever changing hiding places. Despite naval officers, selected from those with experience of chasing privateers, of whom Captain Marryat was one, being given command of the Revenue cutters and the task of catching the master-smugglers, before they could cross the statutory limit of one league and transfer their cargoes to waiting boats, the civil war at sea was no more successful for the Crown than that waged in inland waters; superiority in speed and manoeuvrability, though marginal, was effectively with the smuggler. The Revenue men's only hope of capturing them lay in getting wind of an intended landing on a big scale, through spies working wherever news might be gathered.

While the activities of the Preventative Service was of concern to practically every one in the community, from those afloat or ashore who handled smuggled goods in bulk, to their customers in every walk of society, that other public enemy, the Press Gang, affected seamen not already and properly on a ship's books and thus exempted from impressment, at least for the time being, and landsmen who had the physique, regardless of their willingness, for a life in HM ships, and lastly the wives, children and sweethearts who feared the consequences of their menfolk being suddenly seized and taken away. The Impressment Service had a 'regulating office' in Southampton headed by a Captain with a staff consisting of a Lieutenant, a clerk and two Midshipmen; the 'gang' numbered ten men. With telescopes they watched from the high walls of the town, but they were also watched and when a party of men was ordered to the boats the watcher, abandoning his work, ran and signalled or spoke to the nearest ferryman who in turn made one of the agreed signals, a waving oar, a cloth in the rigging, enough to alert some watcher on the far shore whose hail or rude gong sent those at risk away inland, over familiar field and lane where pursuit would be hopeless. The frustrated Press Gang had also to resort to spies to discover where their quarry habitually went into hiding.

Every stranger entering the parish was therefore considered a possible spy who, if undetected, might overhear enough to indicate that an organised landing was imminent or that the seamen who had escaped the last foray of the Gang were out of hiding and seeking to join a merchant ship short of its complement. So every new face and figure had to be kept under observation, followed and scrutinised closely for some tell-tale garment or other sign, and when the stranger came by ferry he would be cautiously questioned during the five-minute voyage by a native fellow-passenger; if

**The Royal Oak.** Engraving by Philip Brannon (1816-90)/ courtesy *Hampshire Magazine*

he crossed the frontier on foot it would be a vigilant farm hand or a servant at one of the houses who would pass the word. What safer place at which to report and discuss these things than the bench to which none could approach unseen or unrecognised? None would dare interrupt an assembly of elders or of vigilantes at the bench without good and urgent cause. Elsewhere, such as in the busy Royal Oak or in the shadowy alleys between the cottages, none could be sure that careless talk would not enter hostile ears.

Although the strategy and tactics involved in smuggling or in evading the cruelties of service in the Navy were of little concern to the gentry or the professional men resident in the parish there were other weighty matters with which they were concerned and which they discussed in quiet with the elders. On such occasions the bench served a lesser role, a rendezvous to which a servant was despatched to pass the word that his master had something to suggest about the handling of some parish matter which elsewhere would activate a magistrate and then a 'vestry' or parish council, such as provision for the poor and sick. In parishes other than St Mary Extra there were poor rates, lock-ups for the detention of evildoers, and stocks in which drunkards and the like could be put until they were sober or penitent, and there were roads which authority required to be repaired, by unpaid labour, in accordance with the law which, however reluctantly and indifferently the task was performed, did enable regular coach services to link the towns.

St Mary Extra had, under the unobtrusive guidance of gentlemen who elsewhere would have been appointed magistrates and wielded official power, somehow avoided any of these civil matters getting out of hand to the point at which some alien official, some superior authority, was bound to make awkward inquiries. This common concern united in amity the squire and the yeoman, the lawyer and the merchant, the shipowners and the elders who represented the inarticulate labourers, the seamen and the fisherfolk. Compared with many other parts of England, particularly where the labouring class depended precariously on the way millowners put their own interests first and that of their employees nowhere when there was a setback in trade, in St Mary Extra there was mutual respect between every class despite the differences in their wealth and in the ways they had acquired it.

The principal concern of parish vestries, where they functioned, was the unemployed and the destitute poor after any who could be shown to belong to another parish had been turned away. Their barest needs were met by levying on all householders a 'poor rate' which was expended almost entirely in a 'workhouse', a place where the regime was so depressing and repulsive, as it was intended to be, that while there was any way a man was able to keep body and soul together without going to the workhouse, he would take it, be it to work for starvation wages, go for a soldier or turn to crime. But the elders of the virtually independent state of St Mary Extra saw to it that there was no unemployed, no lay-about for whom some sort of a job could not be contrived until he could be put aboard a ship in need of a hand, or an unattached woman could be found a ploy in the fishmarket or sent far down the 'lee-shore' of Southampton River to collect and bring back the abundance of firewood, from wreck and forest, which was thrown up on the beaches after every storm. Nor did the elders see any reason why they should copy other parishes and provide a lock-up or stocks while there were stalwart men to deal preremptorily with any thief or carry away from the Royal Oak a tiresome drunk and dump him under a distant hedge or, if it were imperative that he be made sober and alert without delay, for his own safety, to dip his head in the river. As for the upkeep of through roads, neglect of which on the mail-coach routes could bring down the painful wrath of powerful authorities upon erring parishes, well, there was no through road of any consequence since St Mary Extra was really not on the way to anywhere. The mail-coaches from Southampton making for London other than by way of Winchester, or for Fareham or Lewes, crossed the Itchen some two miles upriver at Stoneham and thence made for Botley, well away north of the parish. The Ridgeway took a little wheeled traffic, it is true, but it served many of the gentlemen's residences strung along the eastern border of the parish, each with its outdoor staff attending to drives, fences, hedges and ditches and their portion of the Ridgeway the condition of which each resident naturally required should reflect his pride and wealth and in no circumstance be less well kept than his neighbour's. Otherwise the parish was traversed by bridle paths and foot paths which, when winter downpours made some part impassable, developed detours as convenient, the original direct routes gradually becoming crooked but footworthy meanderings eventually to become fixed between hedges and fences when the common lands were enclosed. These circumstances not only freed the parish of the collective burden of coach-road maintenance but also from the possibility of urban sprawl which advanced from the gates of Southampton, which was bursting from the tight circuit of its ancient walls, along the roads radiating between north and west. The river barrier which was feared by some was indeed an asset to others, its effect contributing greatly to the attraction of the parish to gentlemen of means seeking a place for retirement or of escape from the Capital. Once the need to cross the Itchen by boat was accepted then all the advantages of the town could be added to the pleasure of living with the amenities centred on Peartree Green. There were not only swift and regular coach services to all the principal cities but also direct sailings to most of the Channel ports and beyond. And there were coffee houses, libraries and dining rooms of the quality demanded by a clientele used to their London prototypes. The town had too an Assembly Room, a Theatre and a Spa, none of large size but sufficient to meet the needs of a steady stream of visitors bent on enjoyment, seeking a cure for their ailments or whiling away the time until they were bidden to embark on a long voyage. The proprietor of one High Street academy, sensing a parental problem, suggested in its advertisement that while Ladies and Gentlemen were staying in the town for the purpose of taking the Spa waters their sons could receive tuition in any chosen subject. Occasionally visitors to the town, always fashionably dressed if not always very distinguished, were rewarded by being joined by King George III. He would walk along the so-called Beach, graciously acknowledging the doffing of hats and the curtsies, giving his subjects a second opportunity by turning about after viewing the upper river and the attractive residences perched up by Peartree Green, and retracing his steps. On one such occasion he agreed with Cobbett that it was a very pretty scene but qualified it by adding "when the tide is up."

The character of life in any English parish at this time cannot be judged without knowing what part the church played, so much depending upon its incumbent. There is no doubt that the inhabitants of the area which eventually became St Mary Extra were religious although the church left its traditional ministrations mostly to the monks of Netley Abbey on its southern boundary. A strand from those pre-Reformation years was woven into the fabric right up to the end of the 18th Century. Every year, on the feast of St Peter, patron saint of fishermen, a procession headed by an image of Peter wound its way in the morning along a long-established route ending at the water's edge where the fishing boats, all freshly oiled with here and there a touch of bright paint, were drawn up to be blessed. To follow the hazardous life of a fisherman was unthinkable without this annual reassurance that St Peter would be at hand in the hour of need. After the Abbey was destroyed and the monks dispersed, any clerk of the new Holy Order not too bothered about the persistence of Romish practice was pressed to lead the procession and to say the prayers, for which he reaped a secular reward in the Royal Oak, at the high table, at the beginning of an afternoon of feasting and merrymaking. Alas, for reasons which will be seen later, at the end of the 1700's religious life was checked and soured by the reluctance of local clergymen to perform any duty at St Mary Extra, and the St Peter's Day procession lapsed.

It was unimaginative and wishful thinking in the Diocese of Winchester which resulted in the country around Peartree Green, to Stoneham to the north, Hound to the east and Hamble to the south, each with its own ancient church and established incumbency, and cut off in the west by a broad and sometimes perilous river, being designated a part of the parish of St Mary in Southampton and the responsibility of its Rector. He disliked the river barrier as much as his new parishioners who had, in order to attend obligatory services, or to have their infants baptised, to hear banns read or to get married, or to bury their dead, had to take to boats, be the weather fair or foul. From time to time baptisms had to be improvised in a cottage by a hurriedly summoned incumbent of one of the neighbouring parishes, lest death come first and deprive the child of a Christian burial. In an 'allegation' to the Bishop, putting the case for a burial ground to be consecrated at Peartree Green it was stated that by reason of the difficulty of crossing the river 'it often came to pass that they had been constrained to bury their dead in the open fields or, if they durst venture over, yet the dead body was followed with so little company as was no way seemly.'

This grievous situation eventually moved a generous parishioner, Captain Richard Smith, formerly Governor of Calshot Castle guarding the mouth of Southampton river, to build a church at his own expense on Peartree Green in 1620 and to present it to the Diocese of Winchester. In September of that year the Bishop, Lancelot Andrews, came to consecrate it and its burial ground and to name it Jesus Chapel. Among the ladies and gentlemen assembled to be introduced by Captain Smith was his great friend the Reverend Dr Robinson who, Smith explained, had been asked to give the customary sermon. The next introduction was Mrs Robinson who, the Bishop was astonished to learn, was the Doctor's third wife. Just why

**Peartree Green and Jesus Chapel.**

From the Victoria County History/ courtesy Hampshire County Library

Bishop Andrews chose to recall a Council of Lyons ruling that a priest whose wife had died would, if he were to marry a second time, be branded as a bigamist and be stripped of his holy office, can only be guessed but whatever it was he considered it an affront to be asked to listen to a sermon by such a transgressor. The proceedings were halted while Captain Smith respectfully argued that that and all other rulings had long been null and void excepting where approved by Parliament, and that one was not; eventually the Bishop agreed to proceed but it rankled to such an extent that his decisions regarding Jesus Chapel left the parish with a residue of problems which continued for nearly two-hundred years. He avoided making any provision for an incumbent or for regular visiting clergymen, deciding that despite it now having its own church the parish should remain St Mary Extra, an appendage to St Mary's in Southampton. There were no volunteers to conduct those offices for which fees were payable for the simple reason that the Bishop had decreed that such fees would not be received by Dr Robinson or any other holy clerk persuaded to come to Jesus Chapel for the purpose but should be paid to the Rector of St Mary's. Not until the early 1800s was an appointment made, a Perpetual Curate at £70 per annum.

The joy in the flock at having at last its own shepherd obscured the consequences for the hitherto *laissez faire* governance of the parish. The first shock came after morning prayers one April Sunday in 1809 when the Curate, the Reverend John Poore, transformed his captive congregation into an electoral body which 'for the better preserving due Order and Regularity in the Concerns of this Parish' elected three members to form a Select Committee, Mr Poore, Anthony Munton esquire and Mr Whitcher, and directed them to meet four times a year 'after morning prayers on the first Sunday following Lady Day, Midsummer Day, Michaelmas Day and Christmas Day, when all persons having any matter of Complaint or other Business should have free access to be heard.' The bureaucratic machine having thus been born immediately showed signs of a future active life; they resolved to buy a box with two locks and keys, one to be kept by the chapel warden and the other by the overseer of the poor, a precaution against possible corruption or theft. They had wisely deferred proposing anyone for these posts lest any might become huffy at the suggestion that he could possibly be other than perfectly honest. The next item was to elect the keyholders of the box which itself was an acknowledgement that officialdom inevitably accumulated papers which would need protection from damp, prying eyes and thieves; the appointments went to Benjamin Bye and Josiah Hunt. Finally, before adjourning until the Midsummer meeting, the Vestry issued its first executive order, in the clearest terms, 'that the Overseer do without delay give such public Notice and offer such a reward as may lead to the apprehension' of an absconder who had left his family a burden on the parish.

The Midsummer meeting heard a report of an investigation into the private affairs of, so far as we know, law-abiding parishioners, a development of parish management under the new order which many had feared; the minute reads 'on a due investigation it was proved that each person acting as Master of a Hoy' (a ubiquitous work-boat used for merchandise and especially for the transfer of goods between harbour quays and ocean-going vessels compelled to anchor in deep water in the offing) 'or proprietor of an open Boat on an average earned at least twenty-shillings per week.' What next would the Vestry think it had the right to do?

At the Michaelmas meeting the overseer reported that he had caught up with the absconder but it seems that the Vestry, after hearing the facts, were not so peremptory in their requirements; the absconder, who may have been a seaman on a voyage which, for one or other of the many causes for delay in the days of sail, ended at Southampton six months later than expected, was simply told that 'he should make a reasonable allowance towards the support of his wife.' And as a burden to all the parish the Vestry at this meeting decided to levy a Poor Rate of two-shillings in the pound, an 'imposition' which most of the stalwarts who directed affairs in happier days had not lived to see.

By the Christmastide meeting the Vestry had abandoned the soundest of financial principles, never to spend money you had not got, which had been followed in the past. They decided to inflict the last indignity on the parish—a workhouse. It was estimated to cost £600, a sum which they decided to borrow on mortgage. Thus ended the first year of Vestry rule.

But one good outcome of the new order should be mentioned before this chapter is closed. During the long years when there was no clerk appointed to St Mary Extra there was no parish register at Jesus Chapel. A child was not properly a Christian unless its baptism was duly registered, nor, it was assumed by some, could a Christian easily pass the pearly gates unless his earthly departure had been properly recorded in his parish church. A custom had grown up which ignored the rule that St Mary Extrans should attend St Mary's in Southampton to register baptisms, marriages and burials. If the state of the river crossing or urgent business affairs made obedience to that rule inconvenient then particulars were written on a scrap of paper and thrust into the hands of the protesting incumbent of Stoneham, Hound or Hamble, depending whichever was convenient for the messenger. Mr Poore ended that custom, which was the cause of confusion to lawyers at the time and to researchers more lately, by providing a register in furtherance of the 'Order and Regularity' he had initiated that Sunday in April 1809.

# 2

# The Cooksey Chronicles

The choice of one particular family, that headed by John Bryer and Ann Bannister, from the dozen or more families long established within sight of Peartree Green, any of which might have provided links with the further characters and events in this history, calls for some explanation but no apology. Perhaps for lack of a scribe or of an articulate storyteller, none other had left the evidence, in national, county and private archives, needed to authenticate the oral history first gathered at Peartree Green and passed down eventually to me by one John Cooksey. He was the spouse of Mary Ann, grand-daughter of John and Ann at the top of the family tree.

Although oral history is generally accepted without question if it has for a long time been fixed by the strokes of a quill, that of more recent origin is apt to engender a degree of caution verging on instant disbelief unless those who carried the history in their heads can be judged as reliable and especially to be free of any ulterior motive. In this case we have to consider three Cookseys: John Cooksey whose sources were his wife, her parents and near relatives, all of Peartree Green; Charles Frederick Cooksey, John's son and a close friend of my father through whom I first heard, as a boy, some tales from Peartree Green; and Charles Frederick the second, from whom I heard his account in greater detail.

The discoveries by Charles Frederick the second, or 'CFC II' for short, at the excavated Roman city of Silchester made little impact on my young mind but the story of his detecting how paper specially made, by a process practically impossible to copy on a small scale, for finishing as Bank of England notes, had escaped from the only papermill that made it and became counterfeits, elevated him in my estimation to the level of Sherlock Holmes. I had no fictional or real hero with whom to compare CFC II when my father read aloud from *The Times* the latest letter from him or from one or other of the art experts who opposed his contention that the coloured wax bust which a Dr Bode had bought in London for £85,000 and had declared was the work of Leonardo da Vinci, was in fact the work of a little-known Southampton sculptor lately deceased. *The Times* deplored the indifference which allowed such a rare treasure to leave Britain to be given a place of honour in a Berlin museum. The art experts and magazines of Europe practically without exception gave of their learning and expertise endorsement of Bode's judgement until, after about six months battle against overwhelming odds, CFC II proposed a practical test be made, in effect to find out what was in the core of the bust, because he had discovered that Lucas, the sculptor, habitually built up the layers of wax, on which to sculpture, over a core of old rags tied with string, so as to save wax. The museum staff eventually constructed an electrically-heated probe with which they gradually extracted a plug of wax from the base. No outsider was present during this delicate operation excepting a correspondent from *The Times* who, Dr Bode thought, would at least report that there was no evidence to disprove that the work was da Vinci's. However, he had to report that the inner end of the 2½-inch square plug had adhered to it a piece of fabric unmistakably from a Victorian bed-coverlet with characteristic raised stitching. (Some of the detail in this outline was not remembered from my boyhood. It came from *The Times,* the whole correspondence and comment being indexed under 'ART, Renaissance, bust, wax (attributed to Leonardo da Vinci and R.C.Lucas)': in 1909, when I was 13.

There were other stories which came to me but were only half remembered from those distant days, such as CFC II's successful battle in the town council to stop the destruction of Southampton's noble Bar Gate because it obstructed traffic, which would better indicate his integrity and perception of historical values than the last I will mention here. It appealed to me, an avid reader of adventure stories in the *Boys' Own Paper,* because he was prepared to adapt to almost any role, near piracy in this case, in order to help the oppressed. In brief, when the French government proposed to sequester the lands and treasure possessed by the Church, CFC II planned and carried through the smuggling of negotiable and other treasure, church plate and vestments, from the Cistercian monastery at Bricquebec in Normandy to Bustard Manor farm in the remote village of Martin in Hampshire. It succeeded, but was a close run thing involving disguise, distraction of the douane and the gendarmerie, near discovery through treachery and finally a chase at sea. Good, exciting adventure.

Ten years, including those of the Great War, were to elapse before CFC II and I actually met. It was at Bustard Manor, the embryo Cistercian monastery, to which the Abbot of Bricquebec had requested him to go at the beginning of the war to manage the farm with local labour so that the monks could return to France and run a hospital for war-wounded then being improvised in monastery buildings. I had ten days leave into which CFC II crammed visits to many archaeological sites, by horse and trap and on foot, from the great Bockerley Dyke down to a small hut-village he had found, and I helped to excavate, on the monastery farm itself. It was obvious that he had used every spare moment he had had while at Martin in the pursuit of his life-long studies as an antiquary. The study of maps and of local legends led him to find a short stretch of stone-paved Roman road deep in a wood, and of field names and local history ended in the pleasing discovery that an English monastery, centuries before, had owned part of that French monastery's land. During these expeditions, along deserted roads, deep lanes and open droves, intermittently accompanied by music unknown to most travellers today, the clop-clop of hoofs against a background of the crushing of gravel under iron-bound wheels, there was ample opportunity to raise questions, at decent intervals and when my host was in the mood, not only about the true adventure stories I had treasured but also about others which my father had mentioned concerning Peartree Green. On one such occasion he deferred an answer until we had returned and had had our supper. In his study he showed me a shelf-full of thick, quarto-sized note books the earliest of which he had begun to fill with his observations in 1883; the latest, half-filled, related to finds and observations within striking distance of Martin, with sketches and plans and cross-references to the Hampshire Field Club Journal and to newspaper cuttings. While I was browsing through that volume CFC II was thumbing through volumes about the middle of the series, finally putting one with an open page on the table. "You ought to find the answers to your questions this afternoon there" he said and left for me to find out. The page was headed 'Taken down from the lips of my Father.' It proved fascinating reading despite its seeming to have no chronological or other order, due to it having been written in snatches at intervals of a day or more, CFC I being at the time an old man and not instantly prepared to continue where he had left off but only to tell whatever his roving memory brought into focus when his son came again with his notebook. There were no illustrations to these particular notes excepting a transcript of an almost blank page in an Admiralty book in the Public Record Office and a newspaper cutting about a ship being launched on Christmas Day 1775 at Itchen Ferry. The text contained a word-portrait of a Captain Bryer, without initials or Christian name, describing his face, stature and dress in great detail.

When I closed the notebook and my host had replaced it on the shelf he unlocked a drawer in his desk, withdrawing a long, baize-covered object. Placing it with mock ceremony before me on the table he opened the wrapping, revealing a ceremonial baton, somewhat like a constable's truncheon but with a regal crown carved and gilt and painted at the top and with a coat of arms emblazoned round the middle. The arms had been designed and painted by William Shayer senior to the order of John

**The Arms of St Mary Extra.**

Devised and painted by William Shayer senior (1787-1879)

Cooksey, CFC II's grandfather, and presented to the same Captain Bryer when he had been appointed St Mary Extra's first representative of the law. This was not oral history nor written history but a solid piece of history from old Peartree Green. Shayer, an expert in heraldry, who had painted many coats of arms on the coach doors of the nobility, had devised a quartered shield, the quarters containing groups of three foaming tankards, churchwarden pipes and fishes, 'all proper' as the College of Arms would say. The dexter supporter was a sailor in contemporary rig, his right hand raised waving his straw hat, in his left a bottle. The sinister supporter was a conventional mermaid with her mirror. The crest was a close arrangement of an eel spear, an oyster dredge and a boat's anchor such as could have been gathered ten times over behind the fishermen's cottages down by the ferry. The motto was carried by a two-headed sea-serpent below the shield, *Quid Rides,* 'at what are you laughing?'

After giving me time to appreciate the exquisite detail, CFC II bid me to take a second look at the shape of the shield. It seemed at first glance to look like any other heraldic shield, perhaps not in exact proportion or curvature for all were subject, within a broad definition, to artistic freedom. This one had a convex top whereas some are hollow; the sides bulged a little in the sweeping curves which turned inward at the bottom to form the usual point—point? it was not a point; it was a blunt rectangle. "Think of a ship" I was told. It became obvious that Shayer had carried his maritime theme right into the basic structure of this unique coat of arms the outline of the shield being clearly the cross-section of a ship, from curved deck down to its projecting keel. "That was not Shayer's fancy; that was something special to Itchen Ferry, like the fishing tackle in the crest, not a ferry-boat or a Hoy or a fishing boat, but a professional smuggler's cutter which, as part of his punishment, the Revenue people sawed in two on the beach" explained CFC II. "I have seen it myself" he continued. "My father took me to see it as a boy. The two halves had been turned into a pair of cottages. We went inside one of them to see the timbers showing above the benches built over the turn of the bilges, and the stern cabin at the back, and the deck-beams overhead. There was a sloping ladder with broad treads and a hand-rope but we did not go up to see the bedrooms. They were made by extending the bulwarks, with clapboard outside and a tiled roof over. I saw them again some years later but had to be content by looking only at the outside. The roofs were rather oddly shaped towards the back, where the bow and stern ends were. There were nets and things stored in the space due to the ends tapering from the midship section. The street front of the two cottages was of brick with ordinary doors and windows, much the same as others in the street. They might be there still; I don't know."

Despite the disparity between our ages we had, during that visit, got on like a house on fire. This was of course mostly due to the warmth and natural hospitality of his wife Maria and himself. I like to think that my genuine interest, as well as a little prior knowledge from another source, in the life and times of Peartree Green helped as well. I was shortly posted beyond easy reach but we corresponded whenever our news was sufficient to merit composing a letter, such as the Abbot of Bricquebec's decision that the political climate in France had changed and that there was no longer a need to contemplate having an alternative establishment in England. CFC II was required to reverse his planning of twenty years before but without the adventure. His next letter told of the results of the sale from which the monastery at Bricquebec had made a good profit just when they needed capital to restore their buildings and renew their plant required for the cheesemaking for which they were well known. The Cookseys had already bought a house in the Isle of Wight and would be moving there on completion of the transaction at quarterday. The splendid views that they had over the western Solent, from the Needles to Dorset, animated with shipping, did not after a year compensate for the tiresome journey to Cowes to board a paddle-steamer to Southampton, or vice-versa, when they wanted to see their friends in that town, or their friends wanted to visit them. On the very day that I reached them at Totland Bay for my only visit there, contracts were signed for the sale of the house. They were returning to Southampton.

From time to time I visited the Cookseys at what was to be their last house. Although in a suburb it retained from its earliest days, when in the midst of fields, an apple orchard. Beyond the orchard CFC II had had a cedar building placed as a study, a retreat, a den. There he had his books, filing cabinet, desk, a large table, chairs and glass-fronted cupboard, leaving all the rooms in the modest house to be furnished and arranged just as Maria liked, unhindered by having to provide space for her spouse's 'toys' as she put it. Invariably during my visits there, after paying my respects to Maria and exchanging our family and domestic news, CFC II invited me to his study to see and discuss some relic he had rediscovered among his packing cases and set out in the cupboard. I am not clear as to just when and where I heard from him the different pieces of the Peartree Green story, and I do not think that matters. I am certain however I did not miss any opportunity to ask him about matters of which he might still have more to tell. These opportunities were not confined to the brief visits to the house but also during our drives in my first car to various places in the county which he wished to revisit. I was not the only companion he had on these visits, for I was not available often enough. It chanced however, when an old friend with whom CFC II had arranged to revisit

Brussels and Bruges fell sick, that I could get ten days leave and take up his friend's tickets and hotel reservations. During that long time he took pleasure in introducing me to art and architectural treasures during the day and to reminisce over dinner at night about this and that in great variety. Of these, three I recall very well.

In the smoking room in Bruges Cooksey remarked that the great oak beam supporting the ceiling-joists had once been part of a ship and showed me how to tell. He went on to say that he knew a village pub in Hampshire, called in fact the Ship Inn, which was full of old ships' timbers. When I asked where it was he said that on the map "it is spelled O-w-s-l . . .". "Usselberry" I interjected in the vernacular. "I spent four or five school holidays there, not at the Ship but a hundred yards up the lane at an old farmhouse."

"Flint faced, thatched like a tea-cosy, next to a big barn with a pond behind."

"That's it" I agreed.

"Early 18th Century, or might be 17th" he added.

This coincidental opening led to an Owslebury story from each of us.

Cooksey recalled his father saying that Owslebury woods and hedges were a principal source of timber for a shipyard at Itchen and another at Hythe. The Hythe shipbuilder had inherited an Owslebury farm but the most convenient route was by wagon to Itchen Ferry and then by water across to Hythe. He would mark the trees to be felled, oak and elm, in the autumn, giving his woodman special instructions how the limbs with crooks should be cut. The timber was barked and rough trimmed. The master-builders and their head shipwrights would go up in the spring, as soon as the tracks were firm enough to take wagon and horses after winter rains, and select the logs and crooks best suited to their expected needs. The wagons going to Owslebury for the timber may well have brought the timbers from an old ship dismantled on the shore at Itchen, for the Ship Inn. The timber was then rough sawn at the yard and set aside to season. A very special Owslebury product for shipbuilding was 'trennels', or tree-nails. These were straight-grained, split oak pegs cunningly whittled down from a rough square, first to an octagon and finally to a sixteen-sided polygon which passed nicely through a metal gauge, the size of which was related to the hole made by the standard auger used by the shipwrights. They came to the shipyard in three standard lengths from which the shipwright chose one a little longer than the thickness of the two timbers being joined, the excess length being cut off flush on either side after the trennel had been driven in to its immovable limit. It has been claimed that because the ridges bit into the timbers, trennels were better than their iron or copper successors.

My contribution to our talk about Owslebury concerned the elder of the two old brothers who owned the farm when I used to go there during those summers of happy memory, Anthony Butcher. My father had known the brothers when he was a boy and they young men. Anthony got the reputation of being a weather-prophet superior to any other in the district. He undoubtedly had perfect long-sight but not sufficient to justify the yokels drinking at the Ship to assert that he could see the weather and the waves right out in the Channel beyond the Isle of Wight. Even from his high observation point on the farm, about 400 feet, my father concluded, that was impossible because the downs in the Island went up to 700 feet. He therefore asked Anthony to tell him his secret.

It seems that a sea captain stayed at the Ship or somewhere in the village and came daily to the farm, with his spyglass, which he rested on a particular gatepost from which could be seen ships going out or coming in by the Spithead channel and the upper part of ships using the western Solent. He explained to Anthony the significance of a cluster of ships sailing towards the Needles or outward from Spithead before a stormy spell had really cleared, and of an unusual number of ships inward bound although the weather seemed fair; and of when they carried two topsails, or only one or none at all, and how their angle showed whether they were running with a fair wind or tacking against it. He also told Anthony how, when a new arrival dropped anchor off Southampton the masters of outward-bound vessels would be rowed across to learn what it was like out in the Channel and what the weather signs there had been. He also told him how they all watched the mercury in the barometer and, learning that the Vicar had a barometer in his hall, they went along for a practical explanation from which the Vicar is said to have learned much. After that Anthony was free to go in and check the barometer whenever he wished. The Vicarage garden adjoined the Butchers' apple orchard. Thus, while his rivals were limited to such lore as 'red in the morning is the shepherd's warning', Anthony added to his weather lore the collective wisdom of unseen experts perhaps twenty miles away.

There was a second addition to the Peartree chronicles from Cooksey after he asked what authors I read. He suggested that I read Captain Marryat's *Poor Jack* in which, somewhere towards the end, Marryat had adapted an incident which I had read about in his notebook at Martin, that in which Captain Bryer had his ship seized in Bordeaux during the Napoleonic war but recovered her by battening down the guard and getting to sea on the tide without a crew other than one old man. Marryat had met Bryer when they were living close to one another, Marryat at Fareham while his ship was being refitted at Portsmouth and Bryer in retirement at Warsash on the Hamble River.

Mention of Napoleon led to a third story. Cooksey saw in an auction sale-room a single silver fork. It had an engraved monogram which he thought was the same as that engraved on other table implements in a fitted leather travelling case exhibited at Madame Tussaud's in London. They claimed that it had belonged to Napoleon. One item was missing from a space between the others. There was not much bidding for this single item apparently with no provenance and Cooksey secured it. On revisiting Tussaud's he was delighted when a member of the firm had to agree that the fork fitted perfectly into the empty place in their set, that the monogram was indistinguishable from that on the other pieces and in fact he had no doubt that the fork originally belonged to their set. Cooksey returned to Southampton well satisfied with having an accurate memory, and with the financial profit it had brought him that day. Then he added to the telling of this story something I was never able to follow up; one cannot say to a man forty years your senior "go on, tell me now" when you know that for some reason or other he does not want to. His words were, as near as I can recall, "I could tell you something about Napoleon which nobody will believe, at least not until some new letters or papers are discovered to convince them."

We made only one expedition together after that jaunt to Belgium; it was as we had promised ourselves a visit to Owslebury, he to show me the timbers in the Ship Inn and I the farm just up the lane to view the Island and the Solent, as much as the distant hedges and trees would allow, to which was added a visit to the church and, down an overgrown farm track, the line of stunted yews which marked the site of a Roman road. A picnic lunch prepared by Maria we had at Cheesefoot Head, an elevated site worthy of such a feast. We reached it via Longwood where the trennels had been made. Then on to Itchen in the hope that the Ship Cottages were standing still and finally to Fareham where Cooksey's friends lived in the house where Captain Marryat had lodged.

Ship Cottages were indeed standing. We had no difficulty in finding them, first when inquiring of a man crossing Peartree and secondly by the odd shape of their roofs compared with their near neighbours. Our walking back and forth trying to get a better view of the roof from the rear must have been seen by several of the inhabitants from behind their curtains for when Cooksey knocked at the door of the one he had entered with his father long before, the door of the next cottage and another across the lane opened, but not that which had been knocked. The two women were indeed chary in dealing with strangers, demanding almost with one voice what was our business. Cooksey respectfully explained that he had once seen the ships' timbers inside and had hoped that the present owner would show them to me. Our reception may be judged from the opening verbal shot across our bows—'Wajuwant?" and the final salvo—"She's out an' don't let nobody in anyway," at which we sheered off.

As we retraced our footsteps to the car Cooksey recalled that when he went to the cottages with his father there was an old man sitting at the door mending a net or something. He said, after looking intently at CFC I's face, "I know who you be. You be Billy Bryer." Billy Bryer was, Cooksey told me, a master mariner turned schoolmaster and navigation instructor ashore after a bad accident aboard ship. His school was at Peartree Green and his three-times a week navigation class was held at Hamble. He attained fame and a cartoon, a copy of which Cooksey had inherited and lent to Tudor House Museum in Southampton, when he refused to part with letters addressed to the Postmaster General at a house on the way. The Postmaster at Southampton had, in view of the regularity of Billy Bryer's journeys to Hamble and the mail to and from the sub-office there seldom amounting to a score of letters at a time, made a contract with him to carry the packet delivered to his school on to Hamble. The Postmaster General's instructions seem likely to have been aimed at receiving letters at mid-day, as Bryer on his cob passed on his way, instead of the next morning, but whatever they were Bryer had not been told. He is alleged to have said to the stranger who claimed to be his ultimate superior —"If you were the King himself, sir, I wouldn't part with one letter. My contract is to carry this packet to Hamble, and that, sir," digging his heels into his nag, "is what I am going to do."

At Fareham, after tea, our hostess showed us her collection of Marryatt's books, complete sets of the English editions and the beginnings of a collection of editions in foreign languages. And so home via the chain ferry which had ended, almost exactly a hundred years earlier, the ferryboats propelled by oar and sail across the Itchen. It had been a memorable, happy expedition mercifully not saddened by foreknowledge that it was to be our last.

It was only about a year later that I was sitting in the study behind the orchard with CFC II's elder son, Father Fred, who was home from the Jesuit mission in British Guiana. He and his brother Walter had joined in celebrating Requiem Mass for their father the previous day.

On the shelf were those notebooks, started in 1883 and now closed in 1926. I ventured to ask whether they contained anything which would explain the hint that his father had known something special about the Emperor Napoleon. "Not the Emperor", he replied, "but the Corsican schoolboy who carried with him his country's grudge against the French when he went off to school in France. The old Dad was chary of telling the story because people could only think of Napoleon as a great general decked out in a gaudy uniform and seated on a fiery war horse. At the time he came to Peartree Green he was far from that, so far that anyone who predicted that he would rise to the top in a military career, and turn into a patriotic Frenchman, would have been thought quite mad."

The truth of the story seemed to me, after I had thought it over from what Father Fred then told me, to depend upon the reliability of the memories of quite a lot of near relatives of Mary Ann Bryer, John Cooksey's bride to be, who would have seen and talked to a shy schoolboy who said he was a Corsican but was at school in France. He had boarded at Havre de Grace the packet leaving for Southampton and during the voyage over had sought the advice of the Captain, James Bryer, Mary Ann's father, as to where he should find satisfactory but inexpensive lodging in Southampton. The Captain noted that the boy's English would not get him very far in making inquiries in the town, and that although many there spoke French the boy's French, though more fluent, was peculiar. The master of a passenger ship cultivated a reputation not only for making safe voyages but also for being pleasant and helpful to any passenger needing help or advice. Such care ensured that his passenger list would easily be filled for future voyages. Had this Corsican been older and perhaps with a heavier purse he could have been recommended the Dolphin, the Star or the Bell, inns which accommodated a constant stream of visitors, but Captain Bryer saw that it would not be prudent just to put him safely ashore and wish him good luck. He decided to offer him a bed in his own house at Peartree Green, which is how he found himself eating supper with the Captain and his wife and possibly as many as eight children of whom Mary Ann was the youngest.

During their visitor's stay they learned his name of course, and the name of the town where he went to school, Napoleone Buona Parte and Brienne. One of the elder sisters had made a note of the name and wrote to the boy after his return to France, with what result Father Fred had no idea. Nor could he say how many years later, or at what Napoleonic event, did the Bryers wake up to the fact that they had once had under their roof the future Emperor of the French. The only written note of this realisation, other than what might be somewhere in those unexamined notebooks, of which Father Fred knew would be the baptismal register giving the name chosen by John and Mary Ann Cooksey for their firstborn child; it was Napoleon.

Our conversation, which was to prove our last although I had a letter from Father Fred after he had returned to British Guiana, tailed off into an account of his brief attempt to find answers to the questions I had raised. He had found the registers at St Mary's church in Southampton incomplete where they had survived a fire at the Deanery adjoining. He had talked with CFC I, his grandfather, and found it impossible to distinguish one from another the apparently four or five Captains Bryer of whom two at least owned their ships, one was a privateer and one took Holy Orders. His grandfather came down to the docks to see Father Fred, then a young priest assigned to the mission in British Guiana, sail for Georgetown. He told him that he had, as a boy, seen off from the same dock his uncle Thomas Bryer, the Captain turned Parson, who also sailed for Georgetown. (The letter I have mentioned was to say that Father Fred had visited the Anglican Christ Church there and found Thomas Bryer's tomb in the south aisle. He had been the first incumbent but had survived only a year.)

In recalling what follows, which I have tried to put into his words, I recall too that when in England he taught history and perhaps regarded me as one of his pupils.

"Oral history is of course always liable to have detail eroded in the telling, usually nothing detracting from the intrinsic interest of the story but the missing details may be just those needed for authentication. We mustn't expect them to have thought beyond their own generation and made a tidy record just for our benefit. When these things happened and were part of their everyday life they knew the detail well, had been brought up with it, who was related to who and what each did for a living and so on. They had no need to write it down. This fact means that you should be wary of any story which is wrapped in inessential detail."

I can see him now, seated on the table, swinging his legs back and forth like alternating pendulums, seated on his broad hands and staring through his thick glasses at the orchard. I knew better than to interrupt his thoughts.

"Don't be too hasty and turn down anything just because you've discovered some detail can't be right; put it aside in case some explanation turns up later. I expect you read about Sir William de Crespigny going to France as a spy; well, I looked him up and found that he didn't become Sir William until the war was over; I looked up his father, the first Baronet, but he wasn't William and at seventy a bit too old to go spying. It was from my grandfather that I got the answer first hand. He knew, as a boy, Sir William as a very friendly neighbour in Southampton and he would not have thought of addressing him as anything other than Sir William and quite naturally he would have said Sir William when telling the story to my father to write in his notebook. It would be finicky to say the story lacked truth because of that understandable inaccuracy—it is arguable whether it was inaccurate since he was the man taken to France and, at a later date, was Sir William."

There was another pause, perhaps to let his meaning sink in. The pendulums came to rest and he turned to me again.

"If you are in doubt whether to accept a story, because you haven't enough evidence to check it out, the best thing is to consider whether the originator could have hoped, by inventing it or by twisting the facts, to have gained some advantage—like a thief concocting an alibi. I can't think of anything that John Cooksey could have gained by inventing such a story and telling it only to my grandfather; nor by falsifying what his wife and her relatives had told him. There were too many people in his life who knew the facts and would have corrected him. In the case of the spy story John Cooksey and the Captain who ferried de Crespigny over to France were obviously great friends."

Soon I was again posted abroad. After a year getting used to life on the Equator the war had broken out; it was nearly over when at last I saw England again. There was too much in the present and in the future claiming everybody's time and too little opportunity to allow one's thoughts to escape into the past. I did however step aside for a few minutes on a journey from Portsmouth to Southampton, to see whether Ship Cottages had by some stroke of luck survived. Practically nothing had survived from Peartree Green right down to the shore. It had been levelled by the blitz of 1940 and the rubble had been bulldozed tidily back from the main streets. The main slope from the Green to the shore was green with grass and weeds, making it look much like I imagined it was, from contemporary prints, two hundred years earlier when sheep grazed there. As a woman with her shopping-bag passed me, picking her way towards the ferry, I asked whether she had known Ship Cottages and where they had stood. "Lord bless you, sir, everybody knew Ship Cottages. Nothing left now" she said, pointing to a heap of rubble. "The timbers were all tarred when they were in a ship and soon burnt out. But what nobody knew, until this happened, was that there were smugglers' hidy-holes, like small cellars, under the floors."

Of the Cooksey clan, descendants of John Cooksey, only Canon Walter Cooksey was left. He had stuck to his parish post not far from that prime target of the Luftwaffe, Biggin Hill fighter aerodrome. When we were able to return to the house we had built for retirement, twenty miles from Southampton, Walter Cooksey came for a holiday as often as he could, always taking delight in his lifelong hobby of water-colour painting. The first time I collected him off the train, a little thin and frail, we deviated to see what had happened to his parents' house. There was nothing left but the wooden studio and a few trees nearby. As we surveyed the studio, then looking so very lonely, I mentioned the talk I had had with his brother there before the war, from which I learned that John Cooksey had named one of his children Napoleon, because he believed that Napoleon's visit to Peartree was true and sufficiently remarkable to merit commemoration that way. "Not only John Cooksey" observed the Canon pensively, "at least two others thought and did the same."

During these visits he enlivened us with many an amusing tale of recent events until one felt that none of the horrors of the blitz and the doodle bombs ever came to his parish. Only once did he revert to the distant past and that was to suggest that if ever I had the inclination and the time to ferret out a more complete story of folk on Peartree Green than that which John Cooksey had handed down then I should start by building up a family tree of the Bryers from whom he got his story first hand.

It was a very sad day for us all when Canon Cooksey died. He was ninety. When the natural and immediate shock was spent he left us only happy memories; his Victorian reminiscences, his apt quotations whenever anything odd occurred, his fictitious friend Paddy who, as occasion demanded, made what at first hearing seemed stupid but was in fact a wise comment wrapped in Irish wit. And there were the water-colour sketches on our walls, of birch trees, a sandpit overhung with gorse, from different angles and in different lights.

Of the obituaries which came to hand at the time all agreed that Canon Cooksey had been educated at Basingstoke Grammar School, had been commissioned an Army Chaplain in May 1917 and served on the Salonika front; that in recent years he had been honorary Chaplain to the Guards Brigade Depot at Caterham, school governor, on the County education committee and bearer of other such tasks as well as all those common to the priest of a big parish. What was new to me was their agreement that he had two names in addition to Walter, by which he was invariably known to parishioners and friends alike, Bertrand and Napoleon. So, he himself was one of the three family Napoleons he had mentioned. None of these obituaries ventured to comment on such a name being given to an English child with no claim whatever to French blood.

Twenty-five years elapsed before I was shown what I had missed among the obits in 1955, that written by the columnist Douglas Woodruff, 'D.W.' of *The Tablet.* His first 'revelation' was that the B in Canon Cooksey's initials stood for Bonaparte and of course the N was for Napoleon, a curious case of putting the cart before the horse. By then I had authentic documentary evidence that his second name was Bertrand and I suspected Woodruff had allowed himself to indulge in guesswork.

Woodruff's second statement, which I was prepared to accept subject to checking on the Bryer's family tree, which I had only just begun to assemble, was that the Napoleon tradition originated with Canon Cooksey's great-great-grandfather, captain of a cross-Channel packet.

Finally, Woodruff gave a somewhat different version of the Napoleon story than that which I had had from CFC II and which his two sons augmented. The Woodruff version, for which he gave no source, was incompatible with the other unless Napoleon had come to England a second time, some time after he had graduated as an officer. In Woodruff's words Napoleon 'was interested in a girl in Winchester whom he had met in Paris.' My first reaction was that Woodruff's version was a restructure of the Cooksey story based half on fact and half on assumption but, remembering Father Fred's injunction, I decided that it should be set aside without being committed one way or the other, in case some new evidence came to light.

# 3

# The Family Tree

When their Jesuit descendant tried to grow a family tree from Bryer stock from Peartree Green he found that church records concerning St Mary Extra were not only incomplete originally but had also suffered damage by fire. Happily, since that time, Record Offices have appeared in every county and city for the safe keeping of local records of every kind. Their archivists have done wonders in restoring the tattered and the faded, in deciphering the obscure and in cataloguing the whole to facilitate study. Nevertheless, had Father Fred enjoyed these modern facilities he would still have been frustrated in making his intended first entry at the top of the page, that of the parents of the first of the Bryers to be labelled Captain in the Cooksey Chronicles but without a Christian name by which one could be distinguished from another.

Although John Bryer and his sweetheart Ann Bannister were both parishioners of St Mary Extra, their marriage was not entered in the register at St Mary's in Southampton where it was to be expected among other marriages celebrated at about the same time. The couple, like many others planning their marriage during the previous 111 years since the parish had been given its own church, were faced with a difficult choice though no more than the proverbial impediment in the smooth path of true love. Either they had to find a priest in another parish willing to come to Jesus Chapel, despite his having to give the fees for the wedding to the Rector of St Mary's over the water, or they could accept the possibility of the Itchen being whipped up by storm or veiled in fog on the appointed day, apart from the fatigue and inconvenience of the journeys to and from the church where their Rector could marry them. That the Rector might have gone to Peartree Green does not seem to have been considered by anyone, least of all the Rector himself.

John, a yeoman farmer and therefore a practical man, would have figured that if he could induce the Vicar of Hound, the parish whose vicarage was the closest to Peartree Green, to wed them in Jesus Chapel, it would be well worth having to pay the fees twice over, once to the Vicar and once to the Rector. Then Ann could wear her best finery without fear of saltwater spray or riverside mud. But the path that way too had its obstruction, the Vicar. The good man did not see why he should desert his post at his beloved church of St Mary, which was dedicated in 1250, to be a substitute for the Rector at an upstart edifice dedicated as recently as 1620. Further, to earn the fees only to give them to the Rector would be distasteful to say the least. He would be glad to marry John and Ann, but in his own church.

John's next recourse was to the Bishop of Winchester for a special licence, using broadly the 'allegations' which had been used in 1620 to state the need to build Jesus Chapel. In granting the licence the Bishop, thinking of that perilous river, may have had pity for the Rector quite as much as for the young couple when, by a stroke of his quill, the Itchen was struck out of their problems and John and Ann could now complete plans for the great day, 23rd June 1731, along a clear path.

Compared with the meagre opportunities for the poor to acquire knowledge in the 18th Century, from schools sadly dependent on the dwindling incomes from ancient bequests and threadbare charities, the middle class was well served by private enterprises. In every town 'academies' arose to fill the local need, each with a curriculum made to measure.

One of Southampton's High Street academies was typical; its curriculum was carefully advertised to attract pupils from the widest field. It was so accommodating and elastic that no parent need look elsewhere. Its staff consisted mainly of the proprietor's wife and daughters augmented by part-time specialists in some subjects, backed up by domestics appropriate for the maintenance of that special atmosphere, a blending of gentility and erudition, peculiar to schools competing for custom.

The learned Doctor, who mastered as well as owned the academy, had a facility to advance well beyond the boundaries of the tuition available in the university which had awarded him his status-giving degree. He acquired sufficient knowledge of the sciences, of commercial practice and modern languages to enable himself to teach, or to have the understanding necessary to direct others to do so.

Consideration for local conditions was shown by the assurance that 'young gentlemen' could continue their education while they or their parents were staying in the Town for the purpose of benefitting from the curative properties of the mineral spring at the Spa; while for 'those intended for a career in commerce' there were not only the subjects of banking and book-keeping and the like but also those branches of mathematics essential for safe navigation, a response to those merchants who had suffered great losses through the stranding of vessels entrusted with their goods and had voiced their opinions.

The fees were a matter for negotiation and strictly confidential. Those charged to parents of 'young gentlemen' probably showed a good profit but those charged to the members of the professions, the entrepreneurs, the ship owners and the ship-masters, all those of the top-hatted force which kept the port alive, were more moderate. It is not surprising then that John Bryer's four children, Elizabeth, born 1740, John ('41), Mary ('43) and James ('45), each in overlapping turn, crossed the Itchen daily to attend their academy. John and Ann probably did not foresee the effect of their children learning in fields of knowledge almost unknown at the farm by Peartree Green or of their mingling with others of their age with stimulating ideas and ambitions, but the result was that none of them looked to a future in farming. John as the elder son would normally have inherited the farm from his father, qualifying to run it by taking an increasing share of its management until his father retired. Old John's disappointment must have been great but was mitigated eventually by both his sons taking to a profession which kept them at Peartree Green, his worry for Ann also being lightened as he neared his end by James promising to move back to the farmhouse to look after his mother.

Elizabeth's accomplishments came to the notice of Lady Floyd whose husband, Sir Harry, had been posted to the British Embassy in Brussels. Their children would need a governess. Elizabeth took the post and remained until the family returned to England where, at the age of 23, she accepted the proposal of Nicholas Lucas, an attorney of Portsmouth. The wedding was at the 'fashionable' church of Holy Rood in Southampton High Street followed by a reception in the assembly room of the Dolphin Hotel only a hundred yards away. Little about her sister has survived excepting that she married John Foster four years later in Southampton.

The way to school lay across the Green, from where the clouds over the distant Wight gave the young Bryers portents of the day to come, then by the lane from the top of which they had a bird's eye view of the latest ship building in Mr Payne's yard, its form gradually sinking behind the cottage roofs as they hurried down until, at the bottom, only a single shipwright might be seen, through a gap between the worksheds and the timber stacks, working on some detail.

Young John, and James in his turn, would have subconsciously taken in the daily changes in the scene, gradually connecting the weather with the amount of sail carried by the ships moving on the water. Closer at hand he would be witnessing the growth of a ship, starting from a simple backbone and going through a period of encagement during which he might see in the morning a shipwright select a rough crook from a heap skillfully transformed, on his return in the afternoon, into a shapely knee fastening a deck-beam to a rib. The timbers complete, the planking began, rising more as the days passed until it became the turn of the deck to form. At that stage John would have noticed, as he paused at the yard on his way home, that the older seafarers passed their hands over the hull and commented among themselves just as his father and a client did when they appraised a horse. John's passing curiosity in these things naturally turned to a growing interest in the why and wherefore of ship construction at these unscheduled lessons day by day.

The next stage of the journey, crossing the Itchen and walking along the Beach to the quay by God's House gateway, provided a perpetual presentation of the art of sailing from which the principles would become clear without the aid of blackboard and chalk. In the offing beyond the quay there were always big ships, loading and unloading, a reminder of the ultimate purpose both of ships and of the lessons towards which he hurried into the town.

John made up his mind; he would be a master-mariner, captain of a ship, supreme in authority and responsibility over all who embarked with him, one of the elite whose profession could be entered only by proof of unfaltering skill and courage to a degree found in no other excepting that of a soldier.

From the academy, which had served him well, John went to a naval officer living in the town who was one of the many waiting for a new seagoing appointment. He turned the academy's theory into practice, at first indoors with invented astronomical readings and then from the town quay when the morning sun was above the sea horizon towards Spithead.

James, although only recently entered into the academy, would have watched his brother's progress some three years ahead of him in time but much closer in fact, for they went to the quays together, and into Mr Payne's yard, asking, John asking the questions but both receiving the answers.

Old John, without openly admitting it, had now accepted that it was unlikely that his farm would remain in the family. Sentiment was hustled out of his thoughts by the hard facts of farming. While many farmers were near ruin because of the poor return they got for growing wheat, John had turned to meeting the demand, almost at his gate, for oats, barley, hay and straw to feed the great numbers of horses and asses stabled within the walls of pastureless Southampton. Scores of draught horses and vanners, cart-ponies and pannier donkeys thronged the quays and streets, waggon and stage-coach teams from afar had to be fed during their stay, to which formidable number must be added the riding and carriage horses owned or hired by the gentry and finally the tradesmen's cobs used by master or messenger to save their time.

Feeding and bedding so many, in widely scattered stables, could not be done without the corn-merchants. They organised the collection and storage of fodder and straw from the countryside and the retail sale and delivery in the town. John Bryer found the Itchen more a help than a hindrance to his effecting delivery of his produce in bulk. His broad-tyred carts were driven out from the foreshore as the tide ebbed to go alongside the narrow barges sent by Adams, the corn-merchant, for loading. When the barges refloated on the flood they were worked by long sweeps across to where the canal-like eastern moat gave access, at high water, to the merchant's yard, most of the cargo going directly into the carts of the customers.

Farmer John was used to looking well forward, knowing that next year's harvest would depend upon his knowledge and how well he applied it this year. Before embarking on some change, be it in the rotation of his crops or trying a new breed of animal, he made inquiry to find and to fill any gap in his knowledge. He saw putting his son's future into the hands of a stranger, in an element of which he had experience only on the fringe, a matter calling for the most careful inquiry. He had on both sides of the Itchen friends concerned with ships and sea-borne commerce from whom he soon learned that the first consideration was not the ship but the reputation of its master.

Among the many ocean-crossing ships regularly in Southampton there were only three or four masters recommended to John without reservation, by merchants who had made contracts with them and by young officers who had served under them. Their fees were high compared with those charged by other masters of lesser account who thought that apprentices should pick up everything they needed to know from the mates, but the mates received no inducement and, serving under an indifferent master were likely to be indifferent themselves.

Thus, in a merchant's inner sanctum, the two Johns were introduced to Captain Nathaniel Walker, master of the *Lady Anne,* 318 tons. They liked one another, a sum was agreed and young John was signed on as an apprentice.

When some eight months later John returned briefly and unexpectedly to the farm and told his many tales, young James needed no further persuasion, completing his studies and being apprenticed a year earlier agewise than his brother. They seldom met during the years they were working up to their final rank although each snatched a few days at home whenever they could. But as each became qualified they became masters of Southampton ships, half the tonnage of those in which they had gained their sea experience, and were mainly engaged in filling the vaults of the wine-merchants in the town who were gradually taking the import trade away from London. 'Southampton Port' became to mean the best that came from Oporto and matured in this country.

At this point the amateur genealogist set down the full names of the first of the Captains Bryer made elusive in the Cooksey papers by denying them their Christian names. That was very easy compared with the labour they created by their having thirteen offspring between them. CFC II had mentioned quite a number of them, recounting incidents of no great importance in themselves but which, when checked with information gathered in recent years and from other sources, indicated the general truth of their content and justifying the assumption that those items which, because confirmatory documents have not survived or had never existed, can not now be checked should equally be accredited with the probability that they are substantially true.

Of the seven boys of this generation three became master mariners, two were lost at sea, the remaining two probably were concerned with some local maritime employment, although no specific profession or calling has come to light, the records of their marriages and of the Christening of their children showed that they lived at Peartree Green.

The eldest of this trio of Captains Bryer was Thomas, of whom Father Fred had talked and written to me. He evidently, at least towards the end of his sea-going career, commanded a ship engaged in the West Indies trade since his taking Holy Orders and eventually being appointed as the first incumbent at the newly built church at George Town must have resulted from meetings with the Bishop of Barbados, William Hart Coleridge, nephew of Samuel Taylor Coleridge the poet.

This case of sailor turned parson had a precedent in John Newton who was well known to English mariners on two counts. He collaborated with William Cowper in writing the *Olney Hymns*, Newton's especially being of the simple, direct and vigorous kind best known to seafarers; in Thomas Bryer's cabin there may well have been the *Olney Hymns* alongside his well thumbed Bible. Newton's works more likely to have turned Thomas' thoughts towards a new profession were in prose and based on his experiences at sea. He served under his father as a boy, then as a midshipman and eventually as a mate and finally as a master in English ships engaged in the African slave trade. He was revolted by this inhuman commerce and, on his return home, publicly denounced it, eventually assisting William Wilberforce in the long battle to get Parliament to abolish slavery.

The fourth Captain was Josiah, a younger brother of Thomas and most probably equal with his sister Mary Ann as one of the principal sources of information remembered in the Cooksey papers. John Cooksey wooed and won Mary Ann and became co-trustee with William Mathews, of Peartree

Green, appointed in Josiah's will. Cooksey does not tell of Josiah's seagoing career which would have justified his calling him Captain but it would appear that he gave up the sea and turned innkeeper while still young. We are left to speculate on how he raised the money to enable him to buy The Bell, in Bell Street which led off the High Street at the side of the Star coaching inn, Cooksey's ship-victualling establishment being opposite the Star and only three or four minutes from the Bell. Cooksey wrote that 'Josiah was a notorious character. He was in the habit, when there was no ferry-boat available, of swimming from Crosshouse to Itchen (ferry landing)'.

The last of the Captains was John's son, William, who appears to have Captained one of his father's ships on the packet service to France, *Frisk,* which eventually became a privateer under his command. Cooksey met him after his retirement from the sea and described him as 'a man of more than ordinary stature, of great courage and hardihood. He dressed in a swallow-tail coat with brass buttons. He wore a powdered wig with a cue tied with black ribbons. His complexion was very dark and his eyes dark and penetrating.' He was of course the Captain Bryer concerned in the adventure at Bordeaux, the recipient of the baton emblazoned with the coat of arms and the father of the schoolmaster who affronted the Postmaster General on the road to Hamble.

# 4

# The 'Peartree Packets'

When the brothers accepted command of short-voyage ships only and marriage became a more satisfactory proposition, it was not surprising that they decided to settle at Peartree Green. John with his wife and two children occupied a house of perhaps three storeys, since he could see, and identify through his spy-glass, ships at Spithead or rounding Calshot while at an upper window. This house stood on the western edge of the Green, overlooking the Itchen and, according to Cooksey, was associated with Bordeaux in its name.

James remained with his mother at the old, spacious farmhouse beyond the Green and to the east at the parish edge. Here he brought his bride and eventually eleven children were added to the household. Whether James contrived to run the farm while regularly commanding ships, perhaps by dispensing with plough and harrow and producing only hay for the market, is not known but it is significant that when a map was published, some years later, to show the awards to various claimants under the Enclosure Act, Old John's original acres were divided between James Bryer, Lady Holland, Lady Rumbold and Thomas Lewin, Esquire.

During the days their ships were discharging their cargoes and reloading both the young Captains passed and repassed Payne's flourishing but still small shipyard as they had when schoolboys. They now however did not see the work going on with wondering eyes but examined the hulls with mature insight until one or other conceived a plan which, if successful, could make them independent of the ship-owners whom they served on a voyage-by-voyage understanding.

Payne's Itchen boatyard began with the building of fishing and ferry boats, gradually moving to hoys and such larger craft until the yard reached its peak when Payne concentrated on and became noted for fast cutters of up to 60 tons burthen. These were a development of the latest Revenue cutters which owed their qualities of speed and manoeuvrability

**The Duke of Richmond's cutter *Goodwood*, a triple portrait.**

Painting by Dominic Serres RA (1722-93)/
courtesy the Tipper Collection

to their builders copying the best of the craft adopted by professional smugglers who consistently evaded capture. In some yards on the South Coast the Revenue ordered a replica of a cutter ordered by an intermediary for a smuggler. The two vessels were built side by side and, before final fitting-out, were sailed against one another, the better sailer going to the Revenue who would pay an agreed premium in the event of that originally laid down for the smuggler proving the better.

Most of Payne's cutters were built to the order of wealthy gentlemen for their own private use, not only for pleasure but also in the case of the larger craft for the carriage of goods. Such privately owned vessels were classed as 'yachts', a term which has a somewhat different meaning today. A good example was the *Goodwood* which Payne built for the Duke of Richmond. She was launched in May 1783 and after trials in Southampton River, during which she had her triple portrait painted, she sailed for her home port, Itchenor, under the command of Captain P.S.Bruff. On 5th July the Duke and his family and their servants embarked for their first voyage in the new yacht, to Havre de Grace, at the mouth of the Seine.

Captain Bruff kept accurate accounts, which he brought to the Estate Office on completion of a voyage, of expenditure and receipts concerning the *Goodwood.* Those that have survived cover the ten years, starting with her first voyage and ending in 1793. The outstanding fact which a study of these accounts reveals is that the sloop-yacht *Goodwood* led a double life, more often as a cargo carrier than in her passenger and pleasure role. And she sailed to much more distant ports to load cargo, mostly timber, bricks, slates, stone and chalk required for building on the Goodwood estate, than when the Duke took his family and friends across the Channel on pleasure bent. The outstanding sailing qualities of Payne's designs were embodied in the hull shape and ballasting, and the single-masted fore-and-aft rig; the interior could be fitted and finished to meet the client's requirements. In the *Goodwood* Payne must have given considerable thought to the ease with which the passenger accommodation—the cabin bulkheads and bunks, the saloon benches, shelves, cupboards and table, and the whole of the decorative lining which covered the timbers or ribs of the ship—could be removed and stored on shore.

Bruff's disbursements at foreign ports, in harbour dues, payment for cargoes loaded and for small repairs and for fresh provisions show that he sailed as far as Riga, in Latvia, putting in only at Arendal in Norway to break the voyage, returning there a second time, for timber. Other building materials were loaded at English ports, Plymouth, Swanage, Poole, Portsmouth and London. Visits to Lisbon were made in both roles, on one occasion loaded with 237 chests of fruit and 61 bags of cotton, not for the Duke or his Estate but surely for a merchant who paid Bruff a very considerable sum under the heading of freightage. From Lisbon too, presumably on a voyage for pleasure, modest quantities of port were carried on which Bruff paid the Customs duty in England. Some was defined as 'for His Grace's use' and some on behalf of a guest, such as—'2 dozen Port at 18/- a dozen for Colonel Jones'. Once the Customs levied duty on 'statuary'. Ports entered across the Channel included Calais, Havre de Grace, Rouen, whence it was an easy coach journey to Paris, and Guernsey.

The crew of the *Goodwood,* as shown by the wages account, consisted of Captain Bruff, a mate and three seamen. Between them the Captain and the Mate would have taken the deck watch turn-and-turnabout when at sea, with one man on deck and another at call, the cook generally being excused watchkeeping. The men would have been handpicked to serve the Duke, sometimes almost as household servants and at others in the roles of ship's carpenter, sail-maker, boatman, cook and butler.

The idea which was intended to make John and James masters of their own ships was to establish a new fast packet service between Southampton and Havre de Grace with cutters specially designed by John Payne, who up to then had built somewhat smaller yachts. The main advantage of the cutter over the brigantines and barquentines then on the route would be the ability to sail the twenty-two leagues from port to port in from ten to twelve hours, sometimes better but seldom worse. Travellers by coach already endured twelve hours and more with the briefest opportunities to snatch a bite and stretch their legs.

Those versed in sailing problems will know that the tidal streams in the Channel are across the direct course and that an adverse current can be avoided by making a landfall 'up tide'. This condition has the advantage too of enabling leeway to be cancelled out by 'lee bowing' the prevailing current. Lastly the more prevalent winds were on the beam, the direction which favours craft rigged fore-and-aft. The vessels with which the Peartree Packets were to compete were large enough to carry a family coach on deck and were of considerable draught. They were not fast enough to be reasonably sure of catching their tide at either end and had to suffer a shorter period in which they could enter or leave harbour because of their draught. The possibility of a tediously long voyage, quay to quay, was accepted because the only alternative was to make the long journey by coach to Dover or Calais, especially for passengers who began their journey from the West Country or the Midlands for whom the route to France via Southampton was attractive in terms of time and expense. The planners at Peartree hoped that excepting for a few days when the tides would occur at awkward times they would, from late Spring to early Autumn, never have to leave too early or arrive too late to allow their passengers to get a reasonable night's sleep at either end. This would allow Payne scope to provide a large saloon unencumbered with sleeping berths, a small cabin for ladies and perhaps a few emergency bunks for sick or elderly passengers.

The first of the Peartree Packets was launched from Payne's yard on Christmas Eve 1775. She was named after James and his wife the *James and Mary*, and registered at the Custom House as being owned by James. The report of the launching in the *Hampshire Chronicle* concludes its description of the *James and Mary* with 'and is allowed to be a very fine vessel.' The new service began in 1776, the year that the American Colonies declared their independence. While the war remained centred across the Atlantic the packet services to France continued until there was an uneasiness about the French and advertisements in the Southampton newspapers for the services carried the proviso, not 'weather permitting', but 'War permitting'. In April 1778 a French fleet of twelve men-o'-war left Toulon for America; French ships began to appear in the Western Approaches to hinder troop transports and storeships bound for America, and then privateers appeared in the Channel. The experiment with cutters as packet-boats was over—but not the active career of the *James and Mary.* The French were not averse to export trade continuing; it kept people in work and brought in Foreign currency in gold. The *James and Mary* became a 'cartel' ship, carrying papers issued in Paris and obtained by a neutral embassy. She regularly sailed into Bordeaux and loaded wine. She also sailed regularly to the Tagus for port. Although Portugal was a friendly country British ships had to run the gauntlet of Spanish privateers cruising off the Portuguese coast. With her Revenue-cutter pedigree out of smuggling, the *James and Mary* could evade the Spanish and also the French with whom there could be misunderstanding and delay concerning the authenticity of her cartel documents.

In 1782 the American Colonists and their French allies defeated the British land forces and Britain acknowledged American Independence. Hostilities in Home waters ceased. John Bryer ordered his first contribution to the Peartree Packets.

In 1783 the *Trial* joined the *James and Mary* on the revived service to Havre de Grace. Their ability to save time compared with the service given by the larger, and probably more comfortable, ships was in some measure due to their shallower draught and their Captains' intimate knowledge of the intricacies of the river bottom from Calshot to Southampton. The Bryers had their own marks to augment the few official beacons and their packets made their way at low water long before the masters of larger vessels were prepared to risk running aground. When James retired from seagoing he was asked by the newly formed Harbour Board, charged with improving the navigational and berthing facilities for ships, to become their first Boomage Master, with the task of marking the channel from Calshot to Crackmore Hard on the Test.

*Published Sept.r 1.st 1800 by J. Walker No. 16 Rosomans Street London*

**Opposite: Calshot Castle, with a hoy and square-tops'l cutter outward bound.**

Drawing by the Reverend J. Streatfield, circa 1800

The berthing facilities in the 1780s were little better than they were when the Norman walls and quays were built. Ships anchored in the deep water off the quays, late comers a mile away when the port was crowded, and passengers were rowed ashore. The Peartree Packets however sailed past the anchorage and on into the Itchen to their moorings off the Royal Oak, where ferrymen, warned when a packet had been sighted, drew alongside almost before the vessel had lost way, taking passengers and baggage to either Crosshouse steps, the prerogative of the ferrymen, where porters from the hotels would be ready and, according to the Town Guide, where a palanquin could be provided. Passengers for Peartree Green were even closer to their landing place. This arrangement not only saved time getting ashore but did not vex weary travellers so much as having to land at the quays, where it often was necessary to cross from one boat to another, so limited were the walls and steps, and the jostling which followed in getting through the busy throng and into the town.

In 1790 John added the *Phoenix* to the fleet. His son William would that year have completed five years of apprenticeship and time as mate in the sister ships of the *Phoenix*. The new master mariner joined his father and his uncle to run the three ships now in the family fleet.

The search for facts in writing or print about these three ships proved much more difficult than that for foliage to put on the family tree. All seagoing vessels were registered at the Custom House, generally the nearest to where they were built. The entries in the Register gave the vessel's name and the owner, a description of the hull and rig sufficient to identify her, and its 'tunnage', so spelt because it was calculated in units equivalent to the capacity of a wine tun, a particular size of large cask. When a register kept at one of the Customs Ports, such as Southampton, was filled it was sent to the head Custom House in London for safe keeping. Alas, they were not safely kept for long, a disastrous fire in 1814 consuming most of the registers. If any survived that fire they surely perished in 1940 when the Custom House became a burnt out shell, the interior from roof to vaults becoming but ashes and rubble where the records had been stored.

Nevertheless, information was found concerning the *James and Mary, Trial, Phoenix, Frisk* (ex *Phoenix* or possibly *James and Mary)* and of a yacht of 11½ tons named *Mary Ann,* owned by James and named after his then youngest daughter, born in 1782, and destined to be Mrs John Cooksey. There were a number of small yachts advertised for hire, with a professional crew, for going to the Isle of Wight or farther along the

**Opposite: Itchen Ferry landing hard, with a square-tops'l cutter beached off Payne's Shipyard and at the Bryer Packet moorings a schooner resembling the type developed in the American Colonies.**

Pencil drawing by an unknown artist/
courtesy the Tipper Collection

Channel. The advertisements emphasised that they had 'faithful navigators', an indication that sometimes in the past gentlemen had not been taken to the harbour that they had bargained for.

Both *Phoenix* and *Trial* pose questions which are not answered by the evidence at present available. Ships' names are not lightly chosen. A ship is a living thing and its owner's hopes must not be put at risk by giving it a name of which it cannot be proud, a wanton or illfavoured or ugly name. The name is best when it reflects human joy or aspiration or denotes some purpose or event in which the ship is or was a participant or strives to emulate. Thus the mutual love between James and his wife make *James and Mary* a fair name, as was also that given to the yacht *Mary Ann.* But from what ashes did John's *Phoenix* arise? Did a capsized cauldron of tar catch alight under her while she was still on the stocks and unnamed, or perhaps a conflagration afloat, her original name then being expunged as having proved unlucky?

*Trial* undoubtedly speaks of an experiment, some change from the normal design or practice previously followed, an attempt to overcome past faults. Another vessel, built to the order of the Customs at a yard at Reedbridge on the river Test, was also named *Trial.* Their purpose was to try out an idea expected to improve a boat's sailing ability, the provision of two adjustable keels, spaced fore and aft, instead of the usual one amidships. The trial that John would most likely have made would have been of a vessel in which he had hoped that difficulties experienced in the *James and Mary* had been overcome.

We should remember that while our seafaring forebears had a clear, undisputed understanding of heaven and hell, if any one of them seriously foretold that the shape of a ship's hull and the shape, size and arrangement of her sails would be determined by scientists in their laboratories, let alone that men would land on the moon, he would have been taken to a priest to have the evil spirit exorcised from him, or put into stocks until he regained his reason—courses denied in Peartree parish for lack of a priest or of stocks. We must not with hind sight blame them for not having made more rapid progress in solving the hidden mysteries of the winds and the sea.

The principal cause of trouble and disappointment in a cutter rigged as was the *James and Mary* occurred when the wind was blowing more or less from astern, when the mainsail would be trimmed as far forward as possible. This sail was much wider than it was high, the mast being positioned well towards the bow and the boom was so long that its end swung well out beyond the stern. It does not require a profound knowledge of mechanics to see why there was an inherent tendency to 'gripe', that is for the vessel to try to turn to face the wind, a condition that required excessive helm to keep the vessel on course. Further, this huge sail, projecting far over the side, took the wind out of the fore-sails, the total effect being loss of that speed on which the Peartree Packets based their reputation.

A second potential source of trouble would be the awkward way which had to be adopted, in a single-masted vessel, of controlling the square top-sails. The well tried and universally adopted method used in square-rigged vessels, from coastal brigs up to trans-ocean fully-rigged ships, was to lead the 'braces', the ropes attached to the ends of the yards, through pulley-blocks on the next mast aft and so down to the deck. By pulling the braces on one side while letting off those on the other, the yards and their sail could be swung about the mast to the most effective angle.

In a cutter there was no effective choice but to carry the braces forward and down, but clear above the fore-sails and the jib-stay, to pulley-blocks at the end of the bowsprit and thence back to the fore deck. A cutter's braces, unlike those in square-rigged vessels, took none of the pull of the sail and the top-mast had to take all the strain. It was a design borrowed from Holland.

John and James could not have failed to learn that the Navy, although still using cutters for going to and fro between men-o'-war at sea, sometimes taking captains to a conference onboard the flagship, sometimes carrying despatches and occasionally dashing inshore to observe what ships were in an enemy harbour, they were giving up the square tops'l in them and trying other forms without a yard. They were in fact beginning to retain schooners with the fleet, especially for carrying despatches and important people with maximum speed to distant destinations, of which the best remembered example is that occasion when the schooner *Pickle* was sent to England carrying the first news and report of the action off Trafalgar.

A schooner was not as easy to manoeuvre in a confined harbour, or in twisting channels, as was a cutter, but the harbours of Southampton and Havre de Grace were not difficult; the Bryers' original choice of a cutter for their packet service was not because it was so nippy in manoeuvre but solely because of its speed. It was the professional smuggler who needed both qualities to save his skin.

Deciding between committing his money into the building of another cutter, the type of which John and his brother now had years of experience, or into a schooner in emulation of the Navy, whose needs were not necessarily the same, would have involved not only much inquiry and discussion but finally John going on a voyage in a schooner to see for himself. His first observation would have been the absence of the brutish, skull-cracking, tree-like boom and the vast area of canvas in the single mainsail of a cutter; his second the ease with which the schooner's gaff sails, each half the size of the cutter's though just as tall and carrying a short, light boom, were managed; and finally the simplicity and 'rightness' of the running-rigging of the top-sails. While more helpful evidence continues to evade discovery we are justified in thinking that it was trying out a schooner, and comparing her with the cutter already on the packet service, that prompted John to name his new ship *Trial.* While positive evidence that *Trial* was a schooner is lacking there is circumstantial evidence which compels attention. Firstly, the odd-looking schooner which is the distant centrepiece of the drawing on page 54 is moored where the Bryer packets customarily moored, just upstream of where the Itchen ferry-boats plied to and fro from the curved hard on one side to the Crosshouse on the other; secondly she closely resembles the fast schooners developed on the eastern seaboard of North America where they would have been familiar to friends of the Bryers among the captains of ships trooping or trading to the American colonies, and even to young Thomas, James' apprentice son. It was the business of the Navy to acquire the lines and the dimensions of vessels observed in foreign parts, for the information of the Admiralty, and

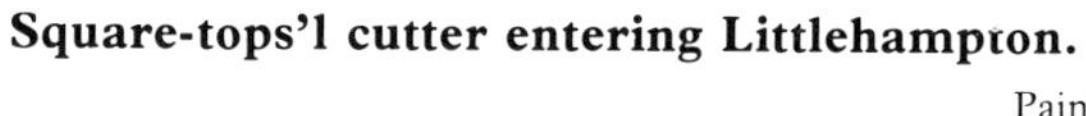
**Square-tops'l cutter entering Littlehampton.**

Painting by William Daniell (1767-1837)

these would be available to ship-builders; thirdly, this American type seemed to have what the Bryers needed for their packet service, speed, with greater simplicity in the standing and running rigging and therefore *Trial* may well have been the outcome of discussions with Payne—and the unknown artist may in fact have captured *Trial* herself with his pencil.

The outlook for the Bryers and of other ship-owners trading with France in 1783, when *Trial* was launched, and seven years on when *Phoenix* was launched, was not overshadowed by the prospect of another disrupting war. France's alliance with the American Colonies had left her unrewarded and bankrupt. Her warships were laid up and her seamen disbanded. Travel to and through France had resumed and was increasing, while essential exports were fetched mostly in British ships. This happy state was not to last; after only ten years, in 1793, France and Britain were at war again, not for a brief period due to diplomatic incompetence but for twenty-two years of fully-armed struggle until Wellington and Napoleon met at Waterloo. By then John and James, who had set out so hopefully in 1775 to create their new, swift packet service, were old men and close to the grave.

# 5

# Alarums and Excursions

When in 1793 news reached Southampton that France had declared war against Britain on February 1st, the paramount topic in Mrs Runacles' coffee house, in Mr Linden's library, at the Dolphin coaching-inn and wherever merchants and ship-owners met was 'how long will it last?' The prophets in Whitehall and the London newspaper offices were no better than any in the principal seaport facing France and the most likely to be affected.

Three-quarters of Southampton's seaborne trade was coastwise in vessels too small to be armed, bringing coals from the Tyne and much merchandise to and from the Thames. The remainder, in bigger ships, whether trading eastwards to the Baltic and Scandinavia or westwards across the Atlantic or beyond, had also to sail along the Channel where, in former wars, French privateers had reaped rich harvests. The Channel Islands alone had up to thirty sloops, few of which exceeded 30 to 40 tons burthen, regularly entering the port with bales of knitted woollen stockings, cattle and agricultural products, and taking back the needs of the Islanders, many of whom were closely related to Southampton families, in the way of hard and soft manufactures essential to sustain them in their isolation.

In their discussions on what profitable use could be found for ships now denied their peace-time employment, they could seek guidance only from their experience of the last conflict with France. The urge was to sustain trade wherever possible despite the large numbers of privateers, manned by audacious, skilful and determined crews, which were likely to swarm again out of a dozen harbours, from Calais to Brest, harbours which were defended as much by intricate, rock-strewn channels as by forts and artillery. An incident which occurred almost as soon as war had been declared could not have been better contrived by Destiny to quicken their thoughts. A French privateer sailed unchallenged by the guns at Calshot

Castle right up Southampton River as far as Hythe. She turned only when cannon balls shot from Netley Castle did no better than sound the alarm.

Had Mr Linden, proprietor of the principal library, with 3,000 books on its shelves, and founder of the *Hampshire Chronicle,* turned back the files of his newspaper to the last year of the last war he could have cited depressing examples of what afflictions the port's merchants and ship-owners could expect. For example, five coasters which had nearly reached safety at Spithead were taken by two French privateers lying off the Isle of Wight; the sloop *Charlotte,* which had loaded with tanning-bark at Southampton and was bound for Ireland, had nearly reached the Irish Sea without being molested, thanks most likely to the skipper's intimate knowledge of the inshore channels and tidal streams along the English coast, when she was taken by a French privateer lying off Penzance; and a local ship the *Bewley* (as Beaulieu was then commonly spelt) sailing from London with stores for Portsmouth was taken off Beachy Head.

In that war, Linden could have reminded them, there had been evolved an alternative to the captor of a ship having to take its crew prisoner and find a prize crew to take the ship to harbour, a task only practicable when the privateer was a large ship with crew to spare and superior armament to ensure that the prize be not recaptured. This was to get the master of the captured ship to sign a 'bail bond' in which in effect the Government acknowledged a debt to the enemy representing the value of the ship and her cargo. In theory the bail bonds held by one belligerent would eventually be offset against those held by the other. It tended to avoid the bloody encounters between boarding parties and desperate defenders, and damage to the captured vessel which often resulted in its sinking or being rendered incapable of being sailed to harbour. The Southampton sloop *Charlotte* was let go after her master signed a bail bond for £200, making Penzance with several feet of water in her hold. But for her cargo of cork she probably would have sunk from the damage suffered in the encounter. The bail bond arrangement saved the damaged ship for her owner and saved the Frenchman from the responsibility for getting the waterlogged ship to Brest. The bigger *Bewley* was ransomed for £1,090.

It is not to be supposed that this gentlemanly procedure had no sinister aspect. Linden could have shown in his files an item which read—'A few days ago a little Dutch privateer took a small vessel not worth £50, but the Dutchman insisted that the English master should ransom the vessel for £200. Upon his refusing, the Dutchman drew his sword and threatened to kill him immediately if he did not sign the ransom bill, which had previously been drawn up for that purpose. The Master, in order to save his life, was obliged to comply.'

To succour the Channel Islanders the Government ran a regular service, notice of which was reprinted year by year in the Southampton Directory until at least 1790—'A swift sailing cutter is stationed here by the Government, in time of war, and sails every fortnight for Guernsey and Jersey, for passengers and small parcels.' Linden had printed a heartening paragraph in his edition dated Saturday March 9th 1782 describing this cutter in action. It reads—'Yesterday the *Childers* arrived from Jersey and Guernsey, with passengers. She sailed from Guernsey on Thursday at one o'clock and was in the Needles yesterday morning at four. There are many privateers in the Channel, but as this cutter is so extraordinary a sailer, none could come up with her.'

If any eager young men advocated clearing the Channel of these cheeky French, by fitting out ships big enough to mount a convincing number of heavy guns then Linden could have provided them with material for cooling thoughts. Two such privateers had been fitted out by Southampton merchants and their backers in 1779, the *Hercules* and the *Childers*. *Hercules* only took one vessel, a ten-gun Frenchman, while *Childers,* which had been commissioned specifically to attack Dutch privateers, was herself nearly taken within hours of leaving Southampton, by a Dutchman cruising off the Needles. Mr Linden was necessarily the soul of discretion, whether writing a leader for the readers of his newspaper or discussing authors and their works with subscribers to his library. In reminding them of what he had printed during the last conflict with France he did not deign to advise ship-owners what to do with their ships or merchants on where to put their money, for these gentlemen were among his clients. As a newspaper proprietor his ear was always alert and receptive and it would have been the current discussions and ideas among those clients which determined his choice of news long past and the timing of its re-printing. In the event there was no proposal to set out another *Hercules* or *Childers,* such merchant vessels being marshalled by the Navy and escorted in small convoys through the danger areas.

The ex-packet vessels in the hands of the Bryers and now lying idle were of the same pedigree as that other *Childers,* the gauntlet runner between Southampton and the Channel Islands and therefore needed no escort. They were free to sail into the Tagus as often as was practicable, for the wine merchants were anxious to build up their stocks of 'Southampton Port' while they could against the ill chances of war. And if the 'cartel' system was revived they could maintain their connection with Bordeaux; indeed there is evidence from later in the war, when advantage was taken to exploit the fact that the Bryers and their vessels were well known to the Bordelais port authority and wine shippers, to indicate that this trade with France was resumed. Since neither Cooksey nor any other examined source mentions *Trial* or *Phoenix* during or after the war there is the possibility that one or both were hired by the Admiralty to help meet the increasing need for auxiliaries of their type to serve with the fleets or with blockading ships. On such transfer the Admiralty sometimes changed a vessel's name to avoid confusion with another vessel on the books with the same name. This practice however tended to confuse historical search, such as when it was found that a hired cutter named *Frisk* was present during Vice Admiral Sir Robert Calder's action against a Franco-Spanish force off Cape Finisterre in July 1805, and in May 1806 joined with the brig *Contest* in landing an armed party of seamen under Lord Cochrane to storm a French battery on Pointe de l'Aiguillon. This elating discovery was however later dashed when further search showed that this gallant *Frisk* had been originally named *Fox* and not *James and Mary.*

There was of course an alternative to laying a vessel up when there was no foreseeable prospect of her being profitably employed—to sell it. Nobody however, not even the Commissioners for Admiralty, were in the market to buy any ship under the circumstances. Although the Navy was always short of ships at the outbreak of war, the Admiralty's policy was to hire a vessel from a port as close as possible to the intended area of operations and, when the operations were over or even when their timing had to be postponed, hand it back to her owner. In that way they avoided having to add to some already overcrowded and overworked dockyard the task of laying the vessel up and maintaining her ready for sea.

At Peartree Green the unlikely did happen; offers to buy, first the little 11½-ton *Mary Ann* in 1793 and then the 53-ton *James and Mary* the following year, came to James Bryer from the least expected quarter, from no farther than Peartree Green. For some time a newcomer to the colony of gentry resident there had been hiring the *Mary Ann,* learning to sail under the instruction of John Bryer's son William who was glad to have something to do now that he was no longer required to apply his skills in a packet crossing the Channel. This gentleman, the youngest of several members of Parliament who retreated to Peartree Green from time to time, was intent on learning the whole art and science of sailing and seamanship, in which respect he was almost unique since most of the not many yachtowners left practically every task to their professional crews, deciding only when and where the yacht should go, taking no active part beyond taking the helm now and then and not taking off their gloves excepting to eat a meal prepared by the cook. This young enthusiast did not spare himself any discomfort nor ignore any detail concerning the why and wherefore of the yacht's construction, the rigging and the sails, ship's husbandry and, not least, all aspects of navigation.

The sale of *Mary Ann* came about when the young man, only a few years older than his instructor, wished to continue the hiring but without an instructor, just one or two seamen who with himself would complete the crew. He wanted to have complete charge, to be responsible for all decisions and thus to satisfy himself that he had the knowledge, skill and confidence to be captain of his own ship. To this proposal James could not agree. After all he had lost a son and a nephew in an accident to a yacht and he knew how easy it would be to lose a life or the ship herself through this young man overreaching himself, venturing too far in deteriorating weather, any of a score of ways in which a simple misjudgement or misunderstanding can in a flash lead to disaster. Very well then, would he sell the *Mary Ann?*

The new owner sailed the *Mary Ann* as its master throughout 1793 and well through the next year, when he sold it to a third owner of whom the only record is that he raced the *Mary Ann* against another yacht for a wager. This transaction was no doubt to help raise the price of his next yacht, the *James and Mary,* the name of which he changed to *Frisk.* He engaged William Bryer as his sailing master and a crew picked from the seamen who had served under Bryer in the packets.

The amount of capital involved in these transactions should not be taken as implying the possession of great wealth by the purchaser. The cost of comparable vessels has been elusive and the best indication is the price paid for a vessel, the sloop *Algernon* whose tonnage at 21 was between that of the *Mary Ann* and the *James and Mary.* This yacht, fitted out and lying in Southampton River, newly built by William Richards at Hythe, cost Colonel James Douglas, who lived at Hook, on the Hamble, £231 in the same year that the *James and Mary* was completed.

These transactions were not between strangers, the Bryer Captains having had some very confidential business with John Henry Petty, MP for Chipping Wycombe, in 1789. In that year English packets approaching the quays at Havre de Grace were met by a waiting throng of people standing perilously at the edge and attempting to embark before the vessels were safely alongside. There were not the customary officials about to exercise control and to take their dues, only a noisy and unruly rabble engaged in interfering with the confused travellers, questioning them, jostling them and often snatching their valuables. The revolutionaries in Paris were indulging in a horrible and bloody orgy from which, while British visitors were prudently attempting to return to their homeland, members of the French nobility were fleeing whichever way they could, disguised in sober or even peasant dress and aided by such of their friends who were prepared to risk their own freedom, or by others whose revolutionary ideals could be set aside by gifts of gold.

During the crossing to France Petty had disclosed his plans. He was going on to Paris with his manservant, as he had done on more normal occasions, and hoped to return with a lady and her son whom he wanted to be able to embark without anyone at the quayside realising that they were not English. It was not possible to say when Petty and his friends would be in Havre de Grace and ready to cross the quays to embark; the details would have to be worked out by common gumption and ready ingenuity when the time came. In the meantime whenever a Bryer packet arrived her captain would covertly inform a trusted agent in the town the hour, which depended on the tide, at which the packet would cast off and leave for Southampton, and the probable time the next packet could be expected. In the event, about a fortnight later, Petty and his manservant returned accompanied only by a boy of about four years. They embarked and left France without much difficulty. Arrived at the mooring off the Royal Oak, the manservant, a big fellow, carried the boy up to the Green to the house of Sir Thomas Rumbold, MP for Weymouth, and two days later he and Petty took the coach for London. On the voyage over, when they were making the sleepy boy comfortable in the bunk in the captain's cabin, Petty told the Captain that the boy's father, the Comte de Flahault, had only a few days previously been guillotined in Paris and that little Charles was now the new Comte.

# 6

# John Henry Petty Lord Fitzmaurice

John Henry Petty, son and heir to William Petty-Fitzmaurice, second Earl of Shelburne, of Bowood in Wiltshire, was at birth, in December 1765, given the courtesy title Earl Fitzmaurice. While John Henry was still a toddler his father was planning his future. His education was to be directed to his becoming a great statesman, first under the best obtainable private tutors, then at his father's old college, Christ Church, Oxford and finally by extensive travels, not just the Grand Tour, visiting the principal Courts of Europe and becoming known to and conversing with the princes and their ministers and the ambassadors accredited to them. Few men would have had such an advantageous preparation for high office. To ensure that nothing went wrong with his plan Shelburne attended to every detail and watched closely over his son's progress. Unfortunately, John Henry's mother died while he was scarcely out of his nursery and thereafter his life was dominated by his father.

Two other men shared in the shaping of the boy's education to achieve its designated goal, the celebrated scientist Joseph Priestley and a scholarly dissenting minister, the Reverend Thomas Jervis.

Joseph Priestley, a fellow of the Royal Society, member of the Imperial Academy of Science in St Petersburg and an associate of the Academy of Science in Paris, was head and shoulders above others of his time as a philosopher, experimental scientist, master of languages and a bibliophile. Shelburne, a wealthy man, was his patron and retained him as his librarian and literary companion at an annual salary of £250, with a house on the border of the great Bowood estate, and ultimately a pension of £150 per annum. Shelburne also provided Priestley with a room in Bowood House as his laboratory and it was there that the scientist was the first to discover and isolate oxygen.

**Bowood Park, Wiltshire: the seat of the 1st Marquis of Lansdowne.**

Artist and engraver unknown

This close association, especially in the creation of a library at Bowood which was to excel all other private collections in the Kingdom, gave Shelburne himself increased stature and self satisfaction among the intelligentsia. He naturally confided his plan in Priestley and sought his help in finding a tutor of outstanding competence. Priestley recommended Jervis.

Some have assumed that Priestley also was a tutor to John Henry, and not just an adviser to Shelburne. Great as was Priestley a man of knowledge it does not follow that he had the essential attributes of a tutor beyond his possession of adequate learning. It was important that the good standing he had with his patron should not be adversely affected by any differences of opinion he might have as to how John Henry should be propelled to the heights of statesmanship. Such differences had to be fought out between Shelburne and Jervis, with Priestley acting as armourer to both forces.

Jervis soon realised that John Henry felt the loss of his mother much more deeply than his father could understand. It was not enough to develop a warm, protective friendship for the boy and he pressed Shelburne to agree to have another boy in the house to share his son's lessons. Alone, John Henry was miserable but when a cousin, William Petty, joined him Jervis could encourage mental sparring and a levening of humour into stodgy lessons. In the woods and meadows of Bowood's broad acres the two would leap and climb and explore and joke with the workers instead of one alone being on an invisible lead held by a man nearly twenty years older and bound by dull decorum. To this physical freedom Jervis, who was a philosopher, a writer of *belles lettres* and a composer of hymns and poems, added the freedom to explore the realms of creative thought. Inevitably John Henry began to question his father's opinions and motives, starting a tiny rift in their relationship which widened until it could no longer be concealed, was never healed and became a lasting subject for idle gossip. The crisis came when Shelburne reluctantly realised that his plans had produced not just an obedient schoolboy but a young, independent thinker whose logic confounded old ideas and developed new ones repugnant to Shelburne. The upshot was the ending of schooling at home and a decision that John Henry should go up to Oxford at the beginning of 1783, earlier than was planned.

John Henry matriculated early in February and went into residence at Christ Church a few days later for the Hilary term, plunging immediately into Book 3 of Xenophon's *Cyropaedia* and Book 2 of Livy's *History.* This was the beginning of a special course in the classics, having a distinctly historical tendency, devised by Dean Cyril Jackson for young noblemen with the status and prospects such as those possessed by Shelburne's heir.

Jervis had taken John Henry about England so that he could learn at first hand how industry's raw materials were mined or grown, how they were converted to merchandise, buildings or ships, and how materials were moved by road, canals and by sea. One of these inland tours must have included Rumsey, where John Henry's great-great-grandfather Sir William Petty was buried, Southampton, full of ships trading with the East and West Indies, the Americas, Africa and the Mediterranean countries, and on by hired yacht to see the Naval Dockyard at Portsmouth. On that occasion they may well have stayed with one of Shelburne's friends at Peartree Green, resulting on the beauty of the place being emplanted deeply in the boy's memory.

Where Jervis and John Henry had been on each of these tours, what they had seen, whom they had met were all questions for Jervis to answer but when the young undergraduate was up he had to answer almost daily letters from his father which one writer described as a bombardment of instructions, on what he should do and what he should avoid in every aspect of behaviour which Shelburne could dredge from the memories of his own youth. While John Henry's letters from Oxford showed filial respect there were between the lines signs of impatience. As Shelburne's questions became pointed and personal, the answers hardened sadly.

During the long vacation John Henry, with his Christ Church tutor Charles Hall, travelled to Paris on the first leg of his planned tour. Shelburne had written to his friends there and provided introductions to others of importance. The Court of Louis XVI was not included in the itinerary because *entrée* was accorded not so much to those of rank or office as to those prepared to wear very costly Court dress.

Their London dress was very like the *floc* worn by the *élite* in Paris and was *de rigeuer* for paying the calls Shelburne had enjoined. This 'undress' consisted essentially of a black cut-away coat, a coloured and embroidered waist-coat, white or buff close-fitting trousers and a neck-cloth. It seems that John Henry saw fit to adopt while in Paris some variant of this costume, less restrained perhaps than that from London and more *chic* in French eyes. Our source is imprecise but, whatever it was, it was noticed with disapproval by another visitor from London, the Marquis of Blandford, who was John Henry's junior by three months.

Their last leavetaking done, their final reports from Paris to Shelburne posted, they headed for the next capital in their itinerary, Luxembourg, reminiscing on the way the events, meetings and conversations of the past three weeks and very pleased that all had gone so well. But at Luxembourg there were letters from Shelburne which showed that all had not been well. Shelburne had received a report from Paris which made him remonstrate; his strict instructions had not been faithfully followed. John Henry was dismayed by the discovery that apparently there was no refuge from his father's strictures, no place where an informer may not be. He replied—'It has puzzled me very much to find out why you should suppose that a three-weeks residence in Paris should have converted me at once into a macaroni, an epicure, and a coxcombe.'

To the next letter from his unsatisfied father John Henry replied in words revealing a specific accusation—'With regard to your charge respecting dress, I have only to say that I am not sensible during my stay in Paris, of any neglect of it which you yourself could term a material impropriety.' That did not satisfy Shelburne either and in his next letter he repeated his complaint about John Henry's dress while in Paris and added another, about keeping an accurate account of his and Hall's expenditure. Significantly he ended that letter by urging his son to take care of his health, which suggests that Shelburne was being kept informed by someone in Luxembourg.

Hall, in one of his regular reports to Shelburne, wrote of John Henry's desire to find out from whom his Lordship had learned that he had supposedly been careless in his dress, and from whom that he had been ill, adding that he suspected the Marquis of Blandford.

John Henry's next letter showed how much he was hurt and unhappy in receiving letter upon letter of unabated complaint,—'Let me entreat you to enquire from myself of things which relate to myself. I am rather above extricating myself even from a scrape by lying, and in all events anyone here will tell you that my word is to the full as good as Lord Blandford's.' The letter to which he was replying must have crossed in the post one he had written only three days earlier, so frequently did letter call for letter. 'I had hoped' he wrote from the depths of depression, 'you would not, at least immediately, have mentioned to me so disagreeable a subject as that which occupies the first part of your letter. In the only sense in which I can take it, it gives me to understand that you have no reliance on my word, and leaves me to suspect that something more will be necessary to restore me to your good opinion than the bare performance of the promises you required of me... There is a mistrust in your letter, which distresses me more, and leaves more disagreeable effects than the paltry illness I am just getting the better of.'

Quite apart from this sad, needlessly protracted personal correspondence, John Henry was diligently reporting, in compliance with his principal instructions, all he observed which would interest Shelburne as a statesman, especially conversations with ministers of the governments and members of the courts in Paris and Luxembourg. Of the pleasure-loving court of Luxembourg he had little good to say. He was disgusted with the everlasting gaming, dancing and idleness without any of the conversations with cultured people which he was accustomed to enjoy in England. At Koblenz they found that the elector of Trier was building for himself a magnificent new palace, which caused John Henry to observe, probably with diplomatic restraint,—'I cannot help being of opinion that princes ought to proportion their luxuries to the size and opulence of their dominions, and it seems unreasonable to me that a sovereign who governs two hundred thousand people should have as grand a residence as one who reigns over many millions.'

# 7

# John Henry Petty Earl of Wycombe

Lest it appear, from the way the life and times of John Henry Petty have been told so far, that less than justice has been done to his father, let us note that during the period immediately before and after Petty's admission to Christ Church, when Shelburne was so much in dispute with him, he was one of the most active members, and ultimately the most important minister, in a Parliament embroiled in a tangle of policies of which none was likely to enable Britain to succeed in her war with the colonies in America and their allies France and Spain. It was Shelburne who muted the opposing factions by his oratory and, despite his having few friends and a lot of enemies, succeeded during a short period as first lord of the Treasury in creating enough unity to enable him to give the American colonies their freedom, to draw an acceptable and enduring, undefended frontier between America and Canada and, not least, to negotiate a treaty ending the war with France. In belated recognition of these outstanding services to the nation Shelburne was created Marquis of Lansdowne. His son was abroad on tour at the time and was surprised to read in a letter from the Marquis that his courtesy title Earl Fitzmaurice was to be dropped and that henceforth he would commonly be known as the Earl of Wycombe because, during his absence, he had been elected Member of Parliament for Chipping Wycombe in Buckinghamshire.

Wycombe had reached Vienna on his tour, now accompanied by a Major Green whose military training might from there on be needed to see them through the trackways which were misnamed 'roads' in eastern Europe. They were the guests of Sir Robert Keith, the British Minister at the Austrian Court, who had letters for them brought by the weekly courier from London. It was not until he had opened and read one of these that he learned that he was an MP and that his style of address had changed to

Wycombe. He immediately wrote his congratulation on his father's receiving his Marquisate and continued—'what you mention about (Chipping) Wycombe surprised me not a little; however, I will forgive you for making me a Member of the House of Commons, upon condition you do not go on to make me a speaker in it.' This 'condition' was not just a good-humoured remark, for he had a poor opinion of speeches to which he had listened in the House, not because of any lack of good oratory but a lack of truth or sincerity. Lansdowne however would have taken it as good humour; he was not one to entertain any 'condition' in deciding what his son should do. Wycombe was to speak in the House in due course, whether he liked it or not.

Lansdowne, still worried about how his son conducted himself without the restraint and prompting which he could no longer exercise excepting by courier service, had questioned Wycombe on his handling of diplomatically sensitive subjects in his conversations with the notables he met. To this Wycombe responded—'In all the several conversations I have latterly had on political subjects my system has naturally been to prolong them so as to learn all I could, and to avoid at the same time if possible ever giving an opinion of my own, in the first place lest it should turn out an absurd one, in the next place lest it should be mistaken for one of yours.'

Although only scraps of Wycombe's letters to his father reporting events and observations during the journey through eastern Europe have survived, there are some which he sent back to Sir Robert in Vienna which were no doubt almost duplicates with regard to factual observations. He reported that they had completed their itinerary in Poland, embarked at Danzig and landed at the naval port of Carlescrona in Sweden. While waiting for the coach to take them on to Stockholm, Wycombe and Green strolled round the dockyard and examined the ships 'pretty much in detail'. They judged that of the twenty-nine 74-gun and 64-gun ships-of-the-line, twenty-one were in perfect condition but the rest 'may be considered unserviceable.' They noticed too that work on two important projects had slackened off—enlargement of the port's facilities and the construction of a canal from Gotenburg to Stockholm.

From Stockholm Wycombe reported his meeting the king on several occasions and evidently had his confidence. They had discussed the king's proposed visit to England the next year and the new constitution in Sweden. After making a visit to the museum in the Arsenal, where he had seen the uniform of 'The Warrior King', Charles XII, his successor told Wycombe that he did not believe the popular story, that while Charles XII was himself reconnoitring from a forward position an enemy marksman shot him dead. In his opinion the king had been assassinated.

Wycombe was not so immersed in international politics when writing his reports not to add something in lighter vein when the opportunity occurred. Thus Sir Robert and it is hoped Lord Lansdowne learned of an amusing scandal involving M. de Markoff, the Russian Minister in Stockholm, who was about to return to Russia at the end of his assignment. He had paid some attention to a pretty French actress who was under contract to the Theatre Royal from which the management would not release her 'to return to Paris' because she was drawing big audiences. One morning the citizens were startled by the rumour that the adorable mademoiselle had been kidnapped from her lodging during the night—she was held to ransom—her landlady had been bound and gagged. So great was the clamour that the Chief-of-Police headed the search for the villains—and discovered that M. de Markoff had staged a fake kidnap.

From Stockholm the travellers resumed their unrelenting itinerary—Gotenburg - Copenhagen - Berlin - Brussels - Calais - London, omitting only Holland where the Prussians were investing Amsterdam. It was February, 1788.

Wycombe was off again in June, this time with an itinerary arranged by himself and without a travelling companion, to Spain, Portugal and Gibraltar. Gibraltar posed a problem; ships were not calling there because whatever sanitary measures their masters took their ships were liable to be quarantined at the next port of call. Wycombe sailed from Falmouth to Lisbon and paid his respects to the ministers but would have had only formal contact with the court where the state of the queen's mind was causing concern. Thence by ship to Cadiz where he found a reply to his inquiry to an old friend, a Mr Eden, now at the Embassy in Madrid. He had told Eden of his plan to seek permission at Cadiz to enter Gibraltar by land. Since he had so far not encountered Spanish officials he wrote—'I much wish to be informed how it is normal to accord indulgences of this nature, and am desirous of regulating my journey in this particular in whatever manner you think most adviseable and most respectful to the Spanish Government.' Whether he succeeded in entering Gibraltar or not he eventually reached, via Seville, Lisbon, the last court and capital on his long list.

There was still another tour undertaken by Wycombe before he adopted Peartree Green as a country retreat and enjoyed being master of his own destiny, at least within the sailing range of his yacht. It was to America. It lasted from August to December, 1791, starting at Halifax, Nova Scotia, working southward to St Agostine in Florida, whence he sailed home via Havana. This was not entirely a 'diplomatic' journey, one of Lord Lansdowne's objects being the investigation by Wycombe of the possibility of compensation being paid for lands seized in Philadelphia to which Lansdowne had a claim as successor to Sir William Petty. Wycombe did however change his itinerary in order to meet President George Washington and deliver to him personally a letter from Lansdowne. Wycombe reported this meeting in Georgetown in a letter to his father: 'I was presented to the President soon after my arrival and was advised by Terman, the French Minister, to be myself the bearer of your letter, as he is not approached in form, excepting when at Philadelphia. I hardly ever saw a man more perfectly well bred. He staid at George Town but one day; upon my telling him that I intended to extend my plan, and to proceed to Richmond and Norfolk, he gave me letters for those places in which he recommended me not merely in the usual terms but as the son of one to whom his Countrymen must feel themselves obliged...'

When Wycombe arrived home in February 1792, he was probably the most travelled and the most widely cultured member of Parliament, better acquainted with many of the courts of Europe, and with the new nation across the Atlantic, than any minister and destined, one would have predicted, to be remembered in the Nation's history. The Dictionary of National Biography accords his father sixteen columns, his half-brother and successor ten and John Henry Petty—not one, not even an entry.

# 8

# Wycombe's Voyages

The paucity of evidence concerning Wycombe's activities between 1792, the year he returned from America, and 1805, the year he succeeded his father as the second Marquis of Lansdowne, may well explain why apparently he has had no biographer. Of the references available to the historian too many are not so much 'evidence' as uninformed and very likely biased opinion, or even sheer invention, originally intended to amuse or to amaze whomever was the chosen recipient of this gossip. Such talk flourishes most when the originator thinks that he is safe from information that would refute his tale or render it absurd. And if it is passed on to further hearers prepared to think ill of the subject, or at least not inclined to give him the benefit of the doubt, then gossip gradually assumes the guise of truth. It is now known that information did exist which, had Wycombe chosen to make it public, would have quashed denigratory gossip. Some may think that he was stupidly obstinate; others may well think that he was admirably resolute of purpose.

In seeking an explanation of Wycombe's apparent indifference to barbed tongues, when others would have been enraged and revengeful, we may come nearest to the truth in the Journal of Elizabeth, Lady Holland. Lady Holland was the wife of the third Baron Holland, one of Wycombe's closest lifelong friends, and the vivacious hostess at the celebrated Holland House parties. She had much affection for both Lansdowne and Wycombe who were among her regular guests. Well understanding the lack of warmth between father and son she tactfully avoided inviting them together. She had however tried to arrange 'chance' meetings between them in circumstances, she thought, favourable to their forgetting the past but the well-meant intention rebounded against her. She confided to her Journal—'Lord W is so displeased with me on that, (that now) in his letters he never names me, or does he write, as he used to do, frequently to me. Arduous would be the attempt to decipher Lord W's character. The most predominent feature is the love of *singularity*. His success in that aim is most favourably aided by his possessing innately a large portion of it. He endeavours more to surprise than to please. His sarcastic humour is excellent, the gravity of his manner sets off his wit. It is difficult to ascertain whether he is in joke or in ernest, and he frequently begins seriously a conversation which his love of persiflage makes him end ironically.'

Wycombe was indeed singular, in the sense that he preferred to stick to his own reasoning rather than to conform to tenets or customs which, in his opinion, were in anyway false or unprincipled, a trait which could be traced back to the teaching and example of his tutor, the Reverend Thomas Jervis, during his formative years. It was the root cause of the estrangement from his father who continued to try to impose his will upon an intellect which had reached and passed his own; Wycombe could not have taught an old dog new tricks even if such an idea ever crossed his mind.

A year's further acquaintance served only to emphasise the earlier opinion of Lady Holland when she wrote—'Ld L never dines out, so his coming was a distinguished mark of favour. His character is a monstrous compound of virtues and failings; the world has never done him justice for his ample portion of the former... His temper is violent, and his disposition suspicious; a man with whom it is impossible to live upon an equality, as he expects a deference to his will that few are willing to yield further than his rank and years demand. He is of a noble, generous inclination when he can serve a friend... His disputes with Ld Wycombe ought not to prove him unreasonable, for he has an eccentric and impracticable character to deal with, who is to the full as suspicious as himself and as jealous of control. The collision of two such dispositions frequently kindles up a furious flame, but at the bottom each loves the other too well for the rage to settle into permanent estrangement, but every moment of each of their lives is embittered by interference on one part and resistance on the other... His son (Wycombe), whom he meant to make a tool for his ambition and to live over again in his political career, shuns the line he designed him for, and is an alien to his country.'

Although Lady Holland and of course many others knew that Wycombe was an alien to his country, meaning that he was often abroad, none mentions that he voyaged from the River Itchen in his own yacht, not as an idle passenger but taking a full part in the navigation and in time of war determining the strategy. The nearest possible reference was written by Lord Gower two years after his death:—'After a youth of considerable promise, he became somewhat eccentric in his habits and amusements', a remark one cannot avoid thinking reflects the general ignorance among the upper class of the knowledge and skill required in executing a voyage safely, a business associated with a particular branch of the working class and not comparable with an 'amusement'.

Why did Wycombe indulge in such a singular amusement? There is no doubt that behind the satisfaction he obtained by excelling, in his own estimation if not in that of his critics, in the art and science of sailing, there was the desire to acquire knowledge of a political nature, particularly from troubled areas abroad, to keep his father informed of the facts when many members of both houses of Parliament adroitly used the product of muddled and wishful thinking as though it were unchallengeable truth. Wycombe had been grounded in the art of procuring intelligence, not in the manner of a spy but by discreet and legitimate inquiry, by Major Green during their journey through Europe and later from associates carefully chosen by Lansdowne when he was in Paris in the dangerous days leading up to the Revolution. Lansdowne's biographer, Lord Edmund Fitzmaurice, records that—'During 1789-1790 he (Lansdowne) was kept carefully informed of everything that passed in Paris, not only by his old correspondent Morellet but by his eldest son Lord Wycombe...' Andre Morellet was an economist, a writer on a wide range of subjects and an academician. During that false peace in 1802-3, following the signing of the Treaty of Amiens and the resumption of postal services, Morellet wrote to Lansdowne and inquired after his 'old friend' Lord Wycombe. Lansdowne replied—'I am very happy in both my sons. I have been uneasy about your friend's long absence from home, but I find that he improves considerably in respect to talents and that his mind strengthens. He lives in perpetual pursuit of information, and his mind appears constantly employed, which makes him happy, and what else are we to look for?'

Confirmation of Wycombe's perpetual quest now comes from an hitherto unpublished Government source in Ireland, the trouble spot he most frequently visited. Lansdowne was interested not only in government policy and military action there but also whether there was any possibility of compensation being paid for lands he had inherited from Sir William Petty in recent times and, very remotely possible, for lands in the far south-west, originally ruled in the 12th Century by the Earls of Kerry from whom he was descended in an unbroken line, of which a house and estate remained as an inheritance in wild, rebellious territory far beyond The Pale. In 1797 there was an official stationed in Derry named Hill, whose task was to examine applications from Irish citizens detained by the military to be allowed to emigrate, a procedure welcomed by the government. To a letter he wrote to a Mr Cooke, his superior in Dublin, forwarding his latest list of persons admitted to bail on giving security to transport themselves to America, he added the following footnote, headed 'Private'.

'We have had a curious man here for some days, Lord Wycombe. I know that his visit to this country had been notified to you. In my opinion he is anxious to discover the true situation of the Country in order to report on it to his father and so far enable him to guide his politicks. He certainly has been very inquisitive relative to the situation of this part of the Kingdom so far as relates to its capability of resisting invasion, but he certainly does it (at least I think so) without any idea of mischief, except perhaps to find fault with some supposed neglect of Gov'nt. He has no person with him but an ignorant servant. I deemed it the most prudent plan to be very civil to him, keep him out of the hands of the Democrats, and give him letters of introduction to gentlemen in the towns he is pursuing who would picture to him the state of things to him in their proper colours... Yours &c G.F.Hill. Derry, August 25th... (P.S.) He has gone to (?Thapere), Ballyshannon, Inniskillen, Armagh, Dublin.'

There is apparently no diary kept by Wycombe of these voyages, or log kept by his sailing master, or reports sent to his father, surviving. From scraps of information we learn that Wycombe was in Ireland in August 1797, June 1798, March 1799 and (but not in *Frisk)* November 1803. Government control was very tight in 1798, when insurrection had broken out; Wycombe had to obtain permission to leave for England. 'Ld Wycombe presents his Compliments', he wrote, 'to Ld Castlereagh, and believing that he shall have occasion to go to London for two or three days, requests that he will have the goodness to direct the customary pass to be made out for him. Ld W. proposes embarking tomorrow night or the night after. Thursday, 29 June 1798, 4—5 oclock.' He evidently intended to return that Summer after reporting his findings to his father. It is also evident that Captain Bryer had asked for an early morning departure so that the ebb would carry the yacht well away from the land whatever the wind lacked in force that Summer night; with a good chance of rounding Land's End before the next ebb became slack. On such occasions Wycombe's movements were determined by the phase of the moon rather than social convenience. And when there was a choice of route, such as sailing to Bristol, (as he would have done to see his father at Bowood,) and taking the London coach from there, he would have preferred to sail most of the way for two reasons beyond the pleasure and pride he had in sailing his yacht. Firstly he was becoming deaf and this affliction often made an impression, through his not hearing or mishearing some remark, that he was disagreeable and aloof, a condition which detracted from what little pleasure could be found cooped up in a long-distance coach filled with strangers. Secondly, he believed that a sea voyage was a cure for most ills.

His most ambitious expedition was however made in 1795, before the French threats of invasion and the associated internal unrest made Ireland

Wycombe's principal destination. A general almost unknown, which was not surprising since he was promoted overnight from being a lieutenant of artillery, had been appointed to the grandly-named Army of Italy. It had been roughly handled by the Austrians and had not reached Italy when winter closed in and it was left without a leader, its uniforms in tatters, perpetually short of food and in makeshift shelter quite unfit as winter quarters. This new general was appointed to put all that right and to restore the army's morale ready for a new offensive in the Spring. Wycombe decided that he could sail to Italy and gain first-hand information on how the Italian frontier defences were being prepared and possibly discover what forward preparations were being made by this General Bonaparte.

*Frisk* could not always rely upon being underway and able to avoid privateers off the French and Iberian coasts, or pirates out from the Barbary coast; she had to be armed sufficiently to stop a boarding party coming too close. To obtain small carriage-guns and some swivel-guns, probably on loan, Wycombe would have had to have Admiralty approval and co-operation as such a voyage in a small ship entailed calling at some intermediate ports under British control. The naval dispositions at the time point to his itinerary being Southampton - Oporto (which Bryer already knew) - Lisbon — Gibraltar — the defended natural harbour at Polenza Bay in Majorca and finally the 500 mile stretch to Leghorn. Again there are no surviving letters or log excepting possibly, somewhere in America, Captain Bryer's pilot-book, in which he sketched harbour plans, views from seaward, leading marks for effecting entry and the depths of water and such information. The views were coloured with water-colours. CFC I had it in his possession and lent it to a shipbroker. CFC II told me that it contained sketches of harbours and anchorages on both sides of the English Channel, Cork and Dublin harbours, the Bristol Channel, the Biscay coast, Atlantic coast of Spain and Portugal and a few in the Mediterranean. On his father's death the book could not be found, nor some Admiralty Court documents which were kept with the book in a black wooden box. CFC II traced the shipbroker to Gloucester, where advertisements were put in the local papers which resulted in the conclusion that the borrower had taken the book and papers with him when he emigrated to America and left no address.

But Wycombe had a corroborative 'document' made by the portrait-painter Louis Gauffier in his studio in Florence as a permanent reminder of that voyage. It hangs today in the rooms to which visitors are admitted at Bowood, the home of the present Earl of Shelburne, near Calne in Wiltshire.

The painting deserves close study. Wycombe is posed as though sitting

**The Earl of Wycombe, 1795. Inset (detail): The *Frisk*.**

Portrait by Louis Gauffier (1761-1801);
photographed by the Courtauld Institute,
University of London/courtesy of the Marquis
of Lansdowne

in the garden of one of the villas which were then perched on the steep slope overlooking the harbour at Leghorn, with its recently built breakwater linking the mainland with a small island still bearing an ancient tower-like landmark built to aid mariners approaching the coast. A chart of Italy and offlying islands is held in one hand; it is unrolled and held facing an unseen listener to whom Wycombe is obviously explaining the adventures of the voyage. At his feet is his telescope. Gauffier showed complete mastery of his art in depicting his sitter's face, figure, costume and the foreground, from the immediate impression the portrait conveys, to the meticulous attention to minute detail. It is the background however which links the picture with far away Peartree Green.

Below a splendid sky there is the coastline to the north of the harbour and below that the rocky island at the end of the breakwater with its high mariner's day-mark. Between the island and the nearer shore are the broad waters of the harbour entrance. To the left is a local, lateen-rigged craft heading out to sea and out of the picture, a type of vessel with which Gauffier would have been very familiar and to whose sails he has given that curvature which indicates the strain in canvas and cordage betwixt the invisible wind and the waves being thrust aside by the breasting bows. All that may have been similar to the background used in an earlier picture, shown to Wycombe as a suggestion for the portrait the artist had been briefed to paint. But to be a complete reminder of the voyage of which Wycombe was justly proud the heroine of the story, *Frisk*, would have to be included. Gauffier was not familiar with this foreign type. He had been to Paris but never, it seems, across the English Channel. He would have gone down to the harbour at Leghorn only to find that the sails had been unbent for overhaul, probably at the sailmaker's loft ashore. The spars would be on deck for overhaul and the cordage a mystery in coils. The vessel's *capitano* was English, spoke French within a too-limited vocabulary to explain the top-s'l cutter's rig and knew not a word of Italian. None of the other vessels in the harbour was of the same type. The *capitano* had had a letter from Wycombe instructing him to help the bearer, Gauffier, in whatever he asked to get the details he wanted for his picture. That help came finally, after all other efforts had failed under the bare mast of that undressed alien craft, when Bryer reluctantly lent Gauffier his 'sail-plan', the only record he had, if queries arose in the sail-loft, of the exact shapes and measurements, as chalked out on the floor of the sail-loft, of all his sails.

A sail-plan is a technical scale-drawing, not a picture which a marine artist would conjure from his palette. Everything, spars, sails—all there were in the locker, some for storm, some for light airs as well as her working suit—and her standing and running rigging, was drawn on a single sheet, small sails overlapping bigger sails overlapping the biggest, each attached to mast or stay according to its kind. The fore-and-aft sails were drawn as though they were unnaturally sheeted along the centre-line, the mid-point between one tack and the other, and all the curvature or allowance for 'belly' in the canvas stretched out of them. Most unnatural however were the square top-s'ls which in real life were limited in their ability to be trimmed at an angle from their mid-way position across the centre-line, by the ironwork attaching the yards to the mast and by the braces fouling other parts of the rigging. They too were drawn flat on the paper, the lower or 'lazy' yard pointing aft and overlapping the main. The Captain and the sailmaker well understood the difference between a sail-plan and what the vessel would look like under sail, but Gauffier did not. Which accounts for *Frisk* sailing into Leghorn harbour, her bowsprit just crossing the 'finishing line' drawn from the end of the breakwater, her invisible crew showing splendid disregard for the maritime custom of very long standing of trimming the sails to catch the wind.

General Bonaparte's army did succeed in its task and eventually occupied Leghorn, but *Frisk* had made a timely departure. Whether Wycombe discovered anything which was of value either to the naval officers to whom he reported during the course of the homeward voyage, or to his father some weeks after he had left Italy, would not have been known to the members of his crew and therefore forms no part of adventures retold either on Peartree Green or down at the Royal Oak.

If we accept that Lady Holland's strictures merit no stronger words than she herself used, then the popular impression that Wycombe was a 'wicked' man rests on very few and questionable sources. Published in this century are a bare two words in parenthesis in the index to R.W. Chapman's *Jane Austen's Letters.* The entry reads 'Lansdowne, John Henry, 1765-1809, second (and 'wicked') Marquis of. . .' This seems to have been based on a widely quoted entry in the Farington diary made two years after Wycombe had died and twelve years after the particular visit to Ireland during which it is implied that Wycombe's conduct perhaps merited the adjective 'wicked'.

Joseph Farington made the entry in his diary after his guests at dinner, his fellow Royal Academicians Thomas Lawrence and Robert Smirke, had gone home. Lord Camden had that day sat to Lawrence for his portrait. Camden had talked of the time when he was Lord Lieutenant in Ireland and of Wycombe who was there during the year of the Rebellion, 1798. The significant words were—'Lord Wycombe. . . conducted himself in such a manner, associating with persons who were known to be disaffected and plotting, that the Government thought it necessary to inform His Lordship that if he did not quit Ireland he would be taken up.' That

Camden did not intend that remark to imply that Wycombe should bear some sobriquet, such as 'wicked', for the remainder of his days is shown by Farington's version of Camden's further remarks. It runs—'When the Marquiss succeeded His Father in the title, He became another man in politics, and professed to support the Government. He had to wait upon the King to deliver the order of the Garter which His Father had worn, and His address to His Majesty was such that the King afterwards said that The Marquiss of Lansdowne was the best bred man He had ever met with.'

It is significant that what Camden told Lawrence was private knowledge which Lawrence was unlikely to have learned already, from the newspapers or from some other sitter in his studio. Of the three obituaries in which such an incident as a threatened warrant of arrest would surely be mentioned if it were public knowledge, that of *The Times, The Gentleman's Magazine* and the local *Hampshire Chronicle,* not one mentions it or his visits to Ireland.

At the time of which Lord Camden was speaking the member of his staff at The Castle in Dublin responsible for security, and the recipient of reports from agents and informers watching all suspected persons, was the Under-secretary of State for the Civil Department. He was the same Edward Cooke to whom his subordinate H.F.Hill reported from Derry on Wycombe's presence and intentions the previous year. Cooke would recall that Hill wrote that he was observing the situation 'without any idea of mischief,' and he seems to have had no new information tending to alter the impression that Wycombe, although on the side of the parliamentary opposition in London, was not on the side of the rebels in Ireland and therefore should be allowed to travel about the country like any other law-abiding person, subject only to restrictions imposed by the military engaged in the search for pistols, muskets and pikes in the hands of the rebels.

From the contents of his letters written to Lord Holland, leader of the Foxite Whigs in the House of Lords, Wycombe in his unofficial capacity as Irish correspondent for the English Whigs, evidently travelled not only quite openly but in the style with which he was accustomed in England, from Dublin to the western border of County Kildare where the army were engaged in the arms drive with exceptional determination, using methods which made both Camden and the Government in London uneasy. Wycombe drove in a chaise and four with his personal servant and baggage some forty miles down the high-road, through Naas, the county capital, and through the market town of Kildare until he was stopped at a military check-point at Monasterevin, on the river Barrow which marks the county boundary and where a garrison had been established. He had observed on the way nothing of special interest excepting that on all the houses lists of the names of the inmates of each were posted in obedience of a recently made order intended to facilitate search for suspects.

Of the militia captain who questioned him, Wycombe wrote that he was 'a very plausible young gentleman, advantageous as to his person and correct in his manner.' Satisfied with Wycombe's identity not only as the heir to an English marquis with deep roots in the Irish peerage but also as an Irish landlord, the captain introduced him into the headquarters of the Wicklow militia. There Wycombe was told that the local situation was such that they were liable to be attacked at any moment and that the troops were tired. In fact the militia had been ordered to treat the country as an enemy's country, and further orders were expected to burn and destroy certain parts until the hoarded arms were recovered. Wycombe realised that his host was one of the militia of which there had been justifiable accusations of atrocities the previous autumn and winter. His next letter to Lord Holland mentions the taking of sheep and pigs, and also of wine presumably from the houses of Irish country gentlemen suspected of siding with the rebels. With it he sent a sample of the pike-heads being forged by country blacksmiths, which had been given him by Major-General Sir Charles Asgill who commanded the forces in south-eastern Ireland. Of the troops carrying out acts designed to bring in the arms, working in dispersed groups under non-commissioned officers, Wycombe thought they behaved like 'mercenary ruffians' who had done more to disturb the country than any other sort of miscreant.

When the centre of the tangled web of military action and rebel reaction shifted to Dublin, where Camden's informers and agents predicted an internal rising accompanied by the simultaneous approach of columns from all directions outside, Wycombe returned there as any conscientious professional correspondent would have done. He rented a villa at Sandymount on the shore of Dublin Bay, about a mile south of the river Liffey, which would have been crowded with shipping, but close to where a natural channel and small-boat anchorage came close to the shore where *Frisk* could lay protected from all but easterly winds which in June are usually so light that the gossamer spider can ride them safely. Wycombe evidently chose to face the expected rising, when the loyalist citizens had no choice, for he wrote to Lord Holland saying that 'I have arranged a little plan of defence and sleep with a loaded blunderbus by my bedside... I fear I must, in case of attack, abandon the lower part of the house in which the coachman and footman repose, for you know that we cannot count upon our servants... but I think Charles (his butler) and myself can take a position in the staircase from where we should very successfully annoy an enemy that meditated an invasion of the upper.' However, the rebel leaders in Dublin were surprised and taken and the rebels, after some days expecting orders to come from others, melted away. The peril was considered to be over on May 23rd but Wycombe stayed on for another month in Dublin during which he was plagued with a skin eruption. News of this reached Lady Holland on 30th June when she wrote in her diary—'Ld Wycombe has neglected an eruption. He is under the care of Drs Adams and Hawkins... This disease gives him an opportunity of moralising... A pampered debauchee writhing under gout, a malady brought on by his own excesses, is an object of general pity;... whereas he says a temperate, unoffending person who acquires accidentally a disease conveyed by harmless, innocent contact, is shunned and treated with disgust and contumely.' Wycombe's doctors pronounced him fit to travel a little before news of his trouble had reached Lady Holland since, as we have seen, he applied to Castlereagh, the chief secretary, on the 29th for a permit to embark for the purpose of going to London for two or three days.

In all we know of this particular visit to Ireland there appears to be nothing to suggest that Wycombe ever gave offence to the Government at all, let alone anything so serious as to justify a threat to arrest him if he did not quit Ireland. Lord Camden's alleged remarks made to the portrait painter Thomas Lawrence were erroneous. Remembering that Camden had been working under great pressure and in fact had asked that he be relieved by a man with military experience, some confusion of memory would account for this; it is possible that he knew of such a threat against Wycombe in 1803, which however, if Wycombe's immediate reaction had been known, would not have justified adverse comment.

Wycombe had returned from Ireland, probably by the Dublin packet service and then by coach, a dreary journey from the mainland port through Bath, Calne, Salisbury and Southampton, to Peartree Green, in the late autumn of 1803, having sacrificed the convenience of travelling all the way in his yacht when he had agreed that *Frisk* be employed on a secret Admiralty project four months earlier. In the post on 10th December he received 'a very extraordinary letter' the contents of which, in the absence of the original or a copy, must be deduced from Wycombe's letter which he wrote the same day to Lord Hardwicke, the then Lord Lieutenant of Ireland.

'It is with the most sincere reluctance' he wrote, 'that I find myself reduced to the necessity of calling your Excellency's attention to anything which concerns so unimportant an individual as myself, but I trust that the regard which every man owes to his own character will prove upon the present occasion a sufficient justification for my so doing. I take the liberty of enclosing...a very extraordinary letter...from a man with whom I have had some differences, and one whose motives I am very much inclined to distrust. I pray your Excellency to inform me what I am to infer from rumours which have hitherto appeared to me too extravagant to merit much attention, and particularly to have the goodness to apprize me whether you deem it essential to my credit or to the satisfaction of His Majesty's Government that I should set off for Ireland, which I am ready to do at a moment's notice, however inconvenient it may be. In the mean time I write by this night's post to Mr Addington (first lord of the Treasury and Chancellor of the Exchequor), entreating as a personal favour that he will have the goodness to tell me whether it has happened to him to learn from any source worth attending to, that any misconstruction of my very uninteresting occupations, have rendered me an object of suspicion to any of the persons entrusted by His Majesty with the Administration of Irish Affairs. My uncertainty whether Mr Wickham (chief secretary for Ireland) is in Dublin or in London, prevents my troubling him with a letter similar to this. As nothing of concealment either now attaches or has attached to my position, I presume my Lord, I may take for granted that the story of a Warrant of Arrest having gone forth against me is as false and unfounded as the charge which it implies. It only remains for me to apologise for the length of this intrusion, and to assure you of the very unfeigned consideration and respect with which I have the honour to be My Lord, Your Excellency's most obedient humble servant Wycombe.'

From the fact that the well-informed diarist Lady Holland apparently had no inkling of this alleged Warrant of Arrest and Wycombe's response, from her husband who had his ear close to the Government although in the opposition party and who was in frequent correspondence with Wycombe, or from her friend Lord Lansdowne or direct from Wycombe himself, compels the conclusion that Wycombe had been falsely accused by the (at present unidentified) man with whom Wycombe had had some differences, and that Lord Hardwicke could have given him the assurance he sought, that being the end of the matter.

# 9

# A Peculiar Privateer

When British agents confirmed a rumour that a fleet of barges was being assembled at Boulogne, and transit camps were being prepared in the surrounding countryside, the reverberations reached and alarmed not only the government in Whitehall and its admirals and generals but also the people of every hamlet over whose fields and commons Napoleon's invading battalions would have to be fought if the misfortunes of war deprived English sailors of the chance to defeat an army on the sea.

Barracks and dockyards were roused from their only lately resumed peaceful ways; discharged soldiers and seamen were recalled; the run-down and almost forgotten militia was reformed by local gentry, that in Kent for example being commanded by William Pitt, the late prime minister, a tired man who was glad to accept the sinecure of Warden of the Cinque Ports.

A newly conceived defensive force was created, the Volunteers, units being raised and commanded, like the militia, by local gentry many of whom dipped deep into their pockets when supplies of equipment from the War Office lagged behind the immediate needs of the enthusiastic recruits. Eventually they were trained by regular officers and sergeants to a standard which commanded the admiration of the professionals. Much drilling, marching and firing on the ranges usually culminated in battle exercises, such as that which ended on Peartree Green, 'watched by many of rank and fashion of the neighbourhood', according to the newspaper next day. The invaders were the Ringwood Volunteers and the defenders were the Fareham Volunteers, the two market towns being some twenty-five miles apart with Southampton river conveniently lying between them to provide some of the features of a Channel crossing, including some uncertainty as to where the landing would take place. The invaders marched about fifteen miles under the cover of the New Forest to the Manor of Cadland which stretched along the western shore of Southampton river from Hythe to Calshot Castle. In the creeks lay ready a collection of boats which no doubt were being watched by outposts on the opposite shore. Not until the loaded boats emerged in force and gave some indication of their choice of a landing place could the commander of the Fareham force decide where to concentrate it. The invaders chose the shore most remote from Fareham, just below Peartree Green. In such exercises neither side 'wins', and each side receives a little help or hindrance by the exercise staff officers to ensure that the opposing forces will reach the chosen battleground at the same time. The organiser of this exercise was William Champion de Crespigny, whose father, Claude Champion de Crespigny, the Proctor General of the Admiralty, had formed the Surrey Volunteers and made his son William a Colonel in that force. William lived at Kings Rew, a house which is now but a 'shadow' in an air-photograph of the Cadland Estate, and knew the Forest well and the shores of Southampton river and especially Peartree Green where his friend Wycombe lived and from where he set out on an adventurous voyage the previous autumn.

Napoleon's infamy did more to make every Englishman, according to his resources and ability, keen to help defeat him than any other cause. Wycombe was now often a sick man and suffering from increasing deafness. He therefore could not effectively become a member of the Volunteers; but he had a yacht and a valiant master and crew. Whether he conceived the idea or whether it came from the Admiralty, whether secret discussions were held on Peartree Green or in Whitehall, the facts remain that the Lords Commissioners on behalf of the King instructed the Mayor of Southampton, the Marshal of the High Court of Admiralty and the Principal Officer of Customs in Southampton to form a Commission 'for taking a Declaration and Bail from William Bryer, Commander of the private Ship of War *Frisk*, a Cutter, to the Effect specified in the Schedule annexed'—but the schedule, with no doubt very confidential instructions regarding the intended employment of Bryer and *Frisk*, has not survived.

This initiating document, which was registered at the Admiralty on August the 23rd, 1803, differed from the normal form where letters of marque were to be granted to the commander of an armed vessel intended to capture enemy ships and their cargoes and bring them before the Prize court in which the owners and the crew would expect to receive the value of their capture less a deduction which went to the Admiralty. The purpose of granting them letters of Marque and Reprisals was unequivocally stated 'to take the Ships Vessels and Goods belonging to the French Republic or to any persons being Subjects of or Inhabiting within any of the Territories of the French Republic.' *Frisk* was much too small to capture an armed merchantman large enough to carry a cargo of any value, let alone to carry enough officers and men to spare to make up a prize crew to subdue the enemy crew and safely bring their capture to an English port. The letters of Marque she would carry were to afford some protection under international law, such as it was observed tacitly by France and England, against members of the crew being adjudged pirates and summarily hanged at the yard-arm.

Allowing two days for this 'King's Commission' to be checked by the lawyers and duplicated in the copy-book by the scriveners, a courier would have handed it to the mayor on the evening of the 26th. Another day would quickly pass in preparing the Bail and Declaration documents and warning those who would be required to attend at the Custom House, including John Baring from London, on 29th. The meeting must have been concluded early enough for the courier to reach the Admiralty the same evening. Letters of Marque were granted on the 30th and despatched to *Frisk*, the last requirement before starting on her mission.

The Bail document was dealt with first on the 29th in the office of William Smith, the Collector of Customs, a man whose own involvement in the nation's urgent preparation to defeat Napoleon ensured despatch of the business, for he had raised and now commanded the Southampton troops of Volunteer Cavalry. The gathering included two merchant-bankers, Robert Adams of Southampton, who had often entrusted funds and authority to Bryer to negotiate with the wine-shippers in Bordeaux and Oporto, as he had done with his father John and his uncle James in earlier years; the second man prepared to go Bail for the integrity of William Bryer was John Baring junior, a close friend of Wycombe, son of Lansdowne's financial adviser for both government funds when he had been in office and for his own private fortune, and co-founder of Baring Brothers, the much respected bank in the City of London. The pivot of the meeting, Captain Bryer, and finally Isaiah Galpine, a Notary Public, completed the roll of those essential to the business, but Wycombe accompanied his overnight guest, Baring, for after all it was his ship and his Captain he was committing to the war effort.

The first document, sworn by Adams and Baring 'on the Holy Evangelists' did not precisely say that each trusted Bryer up to the sum of their Bail but included a statement that 'at the present time of being Sworn they are respectively worth more than the Sum of Fifteen hundred pounds over and above all their just Debts'. In considering the validity of assessing ones trust in a man in monetary terms the Admiralty was following a custom established after cases had occurred in which assurances had been given too lightheartedly or without sufficient knowledge. Many novels of the period reflected the risks taken when debts were incurred on the strength of a bill backed by a third party who, when called upon to fulfil his promise, failed in that moral duty. In this case those going Bail were not only men of substance but of long association with Captain Bryer and his family as was Adams, or as Baring was with the owner of *Frisk*. Galpine may have pointed this ambiguity out to Smith, for it was remedied by a footnote to the second document—'And I the aforementioned William Smith the Commissioner aforesaid do certify the said John Baring the Younger and Robert Adams the Sureties bound for the said William Bryer in his behalf to be respectively Security for the Sum of Fifteen hundred pounds of lawful money of Great Britain'. And in comparing three thousand pounds with the risk being taken by the Admiralty in granting Bryer letters of Marque it should be remembered that they were entrusting to his care and skill some of their very valuable agents as well as secrets which if divulged to the enemy could result in great harm.

The second part of the business, a sworn declaration made by Bryer, affords a word-picture of a quality rare in official documents. The details given by Bryer were required not only for the Admiralty's records ready for examination as occasion might require, but also to convince the commander of any of our naval forces encountered at sea, or their captors if they were unlucky, that *Frisk* and her master and crew were British and fully accredited by the British Admiralty.

William Bryer first described himself as Commander of the Private Ship of War *Frisk*, a Cutter of 54-tons registered at Southampton, British built and having a square stern, one mast but no figurehead. He described *Frisk's* armament as consisting of four carriage-guns carrying shot of three-pounds weight and four swivel guns, and in the arms chest there were three small-arms and a number of cutlasses. Her stores included a barrel of gunpowder, fifty 3-pound shot and half-a-hundredweight of small shot for the swivel-guns. She had but one suit of sails and fifty-pounds weight of spare cordage, three anchors and three anchor-cables, a modest enough outfit for any small merchant vessel or yacht sailing on its lawful occasions but prepared to repel boarders whether they be pirates or from ships of the King's enemies.

The Commander went on to name and enumerate his ship's company. His Mate or Lieutenant was Thomas Baker, his Gunner John Blackman, . . . Collis was Boatswain, John Cantal the Carpenter and James Harrison combined the skills of Cook and Surgeon, all of whom rated as officers or 'after guard'. The seamen numbered eight 'of whom one third are landsmen' or hands with little or no previous seagoing experience, as was the manning custom to ensure a supply of seamen for the navy. The seamen were unnamed, which was just as well since some of them were agents, including William Champion de Crespigny on the first outward voyage, who would clandestinely be replaced by others, homeward bound, in the Gironde river.

Bryer's Declaration ended with—'and the Right Honorable John Henry Petty commonly called Earl of Wycombe is the Owner and setter-out of the said Ship.' The scrivener must have been confused and not working from a draft since he wrote first 'John Henry Petty commonly called Lord Lansdowne' but time was pressing and 'Lord Lansdowne' was crossed out and 'Earl of Wycombe' inserted rather than the whole document be rewritten.

There was still another document to be drawn up and signed. It was a sworn declaration by Bryer, Baring and Adams submitting themselves to the jurisdiction of the High Court of Admiralty and committing their heirs, executors and administrators unto their Sovereign Lord the King, citing William Bryer's commitment 'by Force of Arms to Attack, Seize and Take the Ships Vessels Goods Wares and Merchandizes Chattels and Effects belonging to the French Republic or to any persons being Subjects or Inhabiting within any of the Territories of the French Republic excepting only within the Harbours or Roads or within shot of the Cannon of Princes and States in Amity with his Majesty', a formula which applied generally to privateer ships of a size and armament and fully manned for the task described. In this case however a special and secret task taking priority over that described, which *Frisk* was obviously unsuited to tackle, was the subject 'of certain Instructions approved of and passed by His Majesty in Council... therefore nothing be done by the said William Bryer or any of his Officers Mariners or Company contrary to the true meaning of the said Instructions and all other Instructions which may be issued in like manner hereafter...', thoroughly tying up all the loose ends and seemingly providing for all possible contingencies, but in the end simply confirming that the task was to land agents in France and to collect them after they had done their jobs and deemed it necessary to report their findings in person. That was the 'true meaning', not the capture of enemy ships.

Since the Admiralty's special instructions were so secret it cannot be expected that they have survived as a document. Once they were discussed and committed to memory by Bryer, Blackman his lieutenant and the agents masquerading as seamen there was only one safe course to ensure that, if they were captured at sea or the examination at Bordeaux was more thorough than hitherto, knowledge of their true nature would not reach the enemy—to destroy the paper. With no other official documents to hand we must revert to the Cooksey papers, augmented by CFC II's memories and confirmed in one trifle by Captain Marryat. So far as the Bordeaux operation is concerned John Cooksey would not have had to rely upon Captain Bryer's account, which was probably restrained if not secretive from sheer habit, but also from conversations with William

Champion de Crespigny and with John Cantal the ship's carpenter. When Champion de Crespigny decided to contest one of the Southampton seats in parliament after the war was truly finished, he deemed it prudent to spend some of his time as a resident in the town and accessible to the constituents. He already had three residences, one in the New Forest, another in Carmarthenshire and a near-Town house, Champion Lodge in Camberwell. Now he added Anspach House, lately the home of the Margravine of Anspach, situate close to the West Gate and within an easy stroll of the High Street where all the superior establishments of every kind, commercial, banking, social, were concentrated. There he would meet practically everyone of consequence to him as a candidate for election and in maintaining his popularity as a representative in the House. John Cooksey had come a long way since he had left Potterne in Wiltshire, where his father was a yeoman farmer but had an elder son destined to take over the farm, to take up a position under the patronage of Anstey, the tobacco and snuff manufacturer of Devizes. Cooksey fulfilled his promise as a protégé and was advanced sufficient capital to set up a ship-victualling business to meet the needs of the hundreds of ships using the expanding facilities of the port; associated with its offices in the High Street was a retail grocery establishment whose high quality and variety of merchandise made it become a rendezvous for the cognoscenti as important as were the library or the coffee-house a few doors away. It is almost inconceivable that Cooksey would have neglected the opportunities to discuss the affairs in which he was so deeply interested with a man who actually sailed with Bryer on the first outward sortie to Bordeaux and made the appointed rendezvous there six weeks later, returning with his findings and, as we have already noted, reverting to his duties with the Volunteers. John Cantal, he whose duties were to keep *Frisk* afloat by applying all manner of skills in the event of damage by storm, grounding, fire, collision or gunfire, and navigable by fashioning anew or scarphing broken spars or maybe contriving a jury rudder, returned to Peartree Green and was again associated with his old Captain in parish affairs. He could have contributed to Cooksey's knowledge of the adventure, as could probably others who returned from the French prison camps, but Cantal's is the only name which has turned up in the archives of Peartree Green. Negative results from research, aimed at confirming or correcting the Cooksey account, spelled disappointment but not despair since nowhere did any new information cast doubt upon it.

According to Cooksey *Frisk* made two round voyages during the six-week period from Champion de Crespigny being landed at Bordeaux, or maybe somewhere lower down the Gironde, and his re-embarking and resuming his place among the un-named seamen. Assuming that *Frisk* was sailed well away from the French coast so that an evasion course could be taken in any direction if a potentially enemy ship were sighted, and allowing for light winds which occur in autumn, and for some delay in establishing during the run-in towards the Gironde her implied status as a cartel ship, and finally having sufficient time for the formalities with the Chef du Port and the negotiations with the wine-shippers to be conducted at the normal unhurried pace, Cooksey's statement is wholly credible. Once the brandy was loaded and the account settled in negotiable gold, *Frisk* would be expected to leave on the next ebb tide in daylight; any delay because an expected spy had not turned up would cause suspicion. That Cooksey did not mention how many further voyages were made or the date of *Frisk's* capture points to what he does mention as coming from Champion de Crespigny himself and not from Bryer. It should be remembered that there was an independent witness of *Frisk's* voyaging, right up to her escape from France, Old Ben. His narration in the Royal Oak would have been more colourful but even if he was tempted to it is unlikely that he would deviate from the basic facts since Captain Bryer and Mr Champion de Crespigny were in the locality with their own accounts. The prisoners left behind at Bordeaux did not return, so far as we know, until after a dozen years had elapsed and memories were overlaid with those of life as a prisoner, which, like that of French prisoners in England, was more tedious than harsh. Of these Cooksey, or perhaps more likely his wife, would have occasion to talk over the adventures with John Cantel.

Having regard firstly to the average weather in the Bay of Biscay in the autumn months as determining when the owners of *Frisk* and her like would decide that it was time to suspend the Bordeaux trade until the next year, and secondly that the Navy was contemplating more aggressive tactics against the coastal traffic which kept close inshore along the French and Spanish coasts, it can be reasonably estimated that the capture of *Frisk* and her subsequent escape occurred near the end of October 1803. She was challenged by an incoming vessel flying the French flag not far off the estuary. Whether the captain was unaware of the cartel traffic permitted with Bordeaux or had spotted something about *Frisk* or her crew which belied her supposed status, or as has been suggested he had just had a brush with the British navy and was making for safety when he was affronted by the British flag and, being understandably in a vengeful mood, ordered *Frisk* back to Bordeaux to help counterbalance his having fled from a superior enemy, we now cannot know. We cannot doubt however that Bryer and his company found themselves prisoners; whatever story their captor told.

The gendarmerie, not the military, took the matter in hand and decided to keep the ship's company in custody in the town and to put a guard onboard the ship as she lay at the quay. But Bryer protested that he was suffering from an extremely painful attack of gout and should be allowed to remain in his cabin and attended to by an elderly seaman, 'Old Ben'. As there was to be a guard over the ship and its attractive cargo of brandy in any event, these two were excepted from the party of prisoners marched to the Gendarmerie.

'In a few days', continued the narrative, 'Captain Bryer recovered from his attack of gout and finding that the tide was ebbing and the night a moonlight one and that his ship was warped only by ropes to the quay he asked his man Ben if he thought they could get the vessel out. Finding the guard was below, and possibly drunk, the two battened them down, cut the warps and dropped out of the harbour on the tide. When outside, armed with a double barrelled pistol, he overawed the guard and compelled them to help work the ship back to Portsmouth where the guard were handed over as prisoners of war.' A simple statement which in the hands of a novelist, such as Marryat, would flow at least to a chapter's length, but the present reader must visualise the detail according to his acquaintance with the problems which could arise in such a situation.

Of the subsequent employment of *Frisk* Cooksey does not enlighten us, but he relates that there was a finicky legal argument in the Prize Court at Portsmouth where it was claimed that Bryer had not brought home Wycombe's ship, for the French had captured it; what he had sailed into Portsmouth was a French ship which he had captured from the French force in command of it and therefore *Frisk* should be dealt with as a prize. A search of the Court records, which was especially difficult because of the method of indexing, did not result in clarification. Cooksey says there was correspondence with the Crown and the ship was restored to her owner. Wycombe however had been negotiating for another yacht and when the negotiations fell through he ordered another from a West Country builder, his intention being to restore his health by spending some time at sea. The most likely reason for finding no further mention of *Frisk* in association with Wycombe or, as he became, the Marquis of Lansdowne is that such a useful vessel was re-employed by the Admiralty in a location where Bryer was unlikely to become a prisoner of the French a second time, such as in Irish waters. Her noble owner died six years before the end of the war. If the ship survived until the end of the war then she could well have been restored as a gentleman's yacht and, still named *Frisk,* joined the fleet of the Royal Yacht Club (later renamed Royal Yacht Squadron) based at Cowes.

# 10

# John Henry Petty Marquis of Lansdowne

A very few had sufficient title to go onboard *Frisk* to say farewell that last day of August 1803. Adams and the Admiralty courier from the Crosshouse side, in the merchant's distinctively-painted boat rowed by the only liveried oarsman on the river other than the Mayor's; the inseparable John and James in a second boat, rowed by the Captain's son William, just past his tenth birthday and very proud to have been permitted to take his grandfather and his great uncle on this special occasion; and Baring and Wycombe in a third boat rowed by Wycombe's regular coxswain, glum-faced because he had had to give his place in the crew to some strange 'foreigner' from London who didn't know the difference between a bulwark and a belaying-pin. Some impromptu banter filled the passing minutes when words were lacking to say what each felt, much of it aimed at Captain James who had been appointed Boomage Master to Southampton's newly created Harbour Board, to be responsible for the navigational buoys and perches from Calshot to Cracknore Hard, the joke being that John and James between them had first set most of them up to enable their packets to carry on when other vessels were stuck at low water in Southampton river.

The emergence of the Captain and the Admiralty man from the after cabin was a signal for a hasty shaking of hands and a kiss for young William as the visitors slid over the bulwarks into their boats and drew away. A knot of women and children waiting in the kindly shade of the great oak waved and wept as the sails rose and gave life to the ship. As Wycombe watched his yacht, the heart of many satisfying memories, diminish in his sight he began to realise that he would have to substitute some new interest for her. Any idea of his having nothing worthwhile to do either at his unpretentious retreat at Peartree Green or in London, where his residence was already overfilled anyway with the five Giffard girls and their mother, is quite unlikely to have crossed his restless mind. He would continue to visit Ireland of course, when events there called for an assessment not biased by any of the government's wishful thinking, despite his being deprived of the comfort and convenience of his yacht and having to travel by coach and by whatever government or commercial packet he could find with a spare berth. He needed something new, something constructive which would reflect and satisfy his own peculiar self.

Two things are likely to have directed his thoughts to the project he eventually took up, a fear of failing health and the incongruity of his having to entertain his visiting friends in a private suite at the Dolphin in the town, for want of an adequate residence and staff at Peartree Green. What did they say among themselves when he wished them 'good night' and went from the hotel out into the dark street, walking down to God's House Gate and along the 'Beach' to Crosshouse where a sleepy ferryman was waiting to take him across the water only to face a climb up the rutted way to Peartree Green? He would find or build a house in Southampton, something more appropriate to his social status, more adequate to his domestic needs but without having to sacrifice the convenience for getting afloat in a yacht or the soothing balm of the view he enjoyed at Peartree Green. Not least, it would have to be attainable within the measure of his income which would-be matchmakers considered too small for the heir to a Marquisate and which he had sometimes exceeded through neglecting his father's early injunction to keep careful accounts.

The needs of those engaged in commerce had far exceeded the elasticity of the space within the walls of the town to accommodate more or bigger premises. Existing shops, stores or offices expanded upwards, expelling the proprietors from their living quarters, while new enterprises often had to do with temporary structures which unashamedly used for their back wall the outer side of the Norman defences. The more successful of the business men followed the example of the gentlemen who had built seats on commanding sites on the low hills north of Southampton, building country 'lodges' a mile or two away, their arrival for business each morning in a smart pony-trap giving them a superior air which they would not easily attain while living over the premises. They had at first, like Wycombe now, quartered the town for an existing house or a site on which to build one. But every house of consequence, such as those in Gloucester Square, most hard-fought for by retired naval gentlemen, were entailed property or at least considered too irreplaceable to be let go out of the family. Excepting that the only views those houses had were of themselves, Wycombe might have waited until a short lease could be negotiated and become just another resident in the exclusive Square, giving no

**The 'Castle' bought by the Earl of Wycombe in 1804.**

From a watercolour by Barrow, in the Lankester Collection until destroyed in an air raid. Photograph courtesy Southern Newspapers, Southampton

cause for comment either among his friends or critics, or among the townsfolk. The only possible site which would meet his requirements was that of the old castle-keep at the north-west corner of the ancient walls. It was the highest ground within the walls, on a level with the top of the walls overlooking the river Test, close to a boat-yard and moorings by the West Gate and an easy step down to the High Street. But it was restricted. In the middle was what remained of the old keep crudely converted to a two-storeyed house with a battlemented parapet round its roof. Its circular shape, like a decapitated Martello tower or a lighthouse, was obscured on its landward side by various ad hoc extensions which, with the untidy approach and surroundings, did nothing to commend it as the site for a nobleman's residence. It must have been difficult to come to his decision; it was indeed the only site available in the town but it was so restricted that, like the business premises nearby, the only way to make sufficient accommodation would be to build upwards, resulting in something quite different from the style of architecture then accepted for its elegance and domestic convenience and which we now call Georgian. He decided to build upwards, as high as was necessary to contain all he desired, and, while his architect was about it, to create something outstanding, incorporating some of the features of the castle-like residences he had seen during his travels across Europe. The stump of the old castle-keep with its appendages and untidiness, with an illdefined surrounding lane serving some cottages huddled along the backs of High Street properties but notably, on the sea-ward side, a pleasantly proportioned and situated little residence with a sitting tenant, eventually became Wycombe's property in 1804. The months which the lawyers took to sort out the tangles of title and values were not wasted in the architect's office and work began without delay. From Monday to Saturday it was scarcely possible to approach the site, the narrow streets leading to 'The Castle' being filled with wagons and lesser but equally obstructive vehicles bringing stone and bricks, joists and beams, lime and sand; on Sundays going to see the new castle's progress during the past week became as popular an object for a walk as going to see what ships had come and gone. The young vied with one another in predicting how high it was to be and what the several skyward projections were for; the old just looked and shook their heads.

For details of the architecture and environment we have to rely upon contemporary paintings and engravings in the absence of the architect's plans and elevations, always remembering that as a rule the artists set up their easels where the subject of their work can be seen within an attractive setting and from a point easily attained by those whom they hope will buy prints of their pictures and want to see the scene for themselves. It was not easy for Barrow to depict the comparatively low predecessor of Wycombe's creation, even from, as it has been judged, a high back window of a house in Castle Lane. He would have found it practically impossible five years later to have depicted the new castle soaring up four times as high. To draw it as a whole, and as seen from a stance on the ground where the viewer would not have to crane his neck or imagine that something in the foreground was not there, one would have to go at least half-a-mile away along the shore of the Test in a northerly direction. Excepting from a boat out on the water, there was no other locality from which this singular structure could be seen effectively. On the other hand, from the upper windows or turrets, Wycombe and his guests had panoramic views obstruced only by the spire of nearby St Michael's Church, with the South Downs to the north, the Isle of Wight to the south, his beloved Peartree Green close to the east and, to the west, beyond the Forest, the chalk cliffs of Dorset. Whatever else the critics found to disapprove they could not fault the views resulting from the spectacular height of this latter-day castle.

Early in May, 1805, when Wycombe was pressing for the completion of the interior decoration and cabinet work so that furnishing could be begun, his father died. Although this event could not have been wholly unexpected, since the Marquis was approaching seventy, its consequences changed the assumptions on which he had based his plans to leave Peartree Green and live in Southampton. Wycombe now had the Bowood mansion and its parkland, woods and farms; Lansdowne House in London and a number of outlying estates each with its own lesser but not inconsiderable residence. He looked upon Bowood of unhappy memory, the house which could have contained several of his castles and the estate larger than the whole of Southampton, much as he had regarded those grandiose palaces of petty princes he remarked upon during his European tour. It is unlikely that he ever considered living there again. Lansdowne House was another matter; it was similar to several others which were essential to their owners for the participation of their families in the social round of the London season. Although the new Marquis had shown little inclination in recent years to throw himself into any social gaiety he was persuaded that perhaps a Marquis needed just such a residence even if it were to be more of a symbol than a family residence. Of the rest of the Lansdowne properties none lay near the sea and in his estimation were simply parts of the main source of his future income, to be leased or sold as his estate managers and lawyers advised to meet his late father's debts and fulfil the terms of certain settlements.

The obsequies over, the condolences received, the tiring sessions with the executors and the lawyers nearly over, some of the Marquis's friends prevailed upon him not to return to Southampton until he had listened to and considered their views on his future. They had persuaded him to retain Lansdowne House; they now persuaded him that he needed a hostess in Lansdowne House and a wife to take care of him and of his social affairs. There is very little on record—and there is no reason why we should expect there to be—regarding Wycombe seriously contemplating marriage. An alleged refusal of his proposal in 1792 and a brief dalliance in 1799 seems to be all, but what young lady in her right mind would willingly marry a man devoted to a ship and sailing away in her to trouble spots where, if he was not already drowned en route, he was liable to be arrested—or worse?

At the end of May, in a private house in Mount Street, the Marquis married by special licence Maria Arabella, widow of his old friend Duke Giffard. Because she had been living at Wycombe Lodge with her five young daughters since she had left Ireland the gossips could not resist putting into circulation snide remarks about this unannounced and very private ceremony. Lady Bessborough, in a letter to Lord Granville Leveson-Gower, described Lady Giffard as '. . . a vulgar Irish woman near fifty and larger than Mrs Fitzherbert', adding an admission that she had it only by hearsay. She went on 'I suppose it is point d'honneur for she has liv'd with him publickly as his mistress for some years past.' In fact she came from Wales, the daughter of the Reverend Hinton Maddock. Lady Holland does mention in her diary that on his return from Ireland in November 1798 Wycombe came up to London and called, to discuss with her husband his findings in Ireland, but went back to his house in Richmond afterwards, instead of going to his father's house close at hand. The gossips who took that and similar visits as evidence of Lady Giffard being a 'kept woman' ignored, or did not know, that the Giffard children were in Wycombe's guardianship and that his Richmond house was effectively his only pied-a-terre in or near London.

Not until more than a year of shuttered silence had elapsed since the late Marquis had last passed through its doors did Lansdowne House return to its place among the great mansions which made London, despite the continuing war on the continent, the mecca of everyone, nobleman or commoner, who was anyone because of his wit, or his wisdom or his wealth. In June, 1806, Lady Bessborough, who was no friend of the new Marquis or of his lady, wrote—'Lady Lansdowne gave a most magnificent Masquerade; the garden was brilliantly illuminated, and crowded with Masks and music' *(sic)*. 'The night was hot and we were in the (Devonshire House) Garden. . .', where her thoughts turned upon the death of the Duchess of Devonshire which had occurred some eleven weeks earlier, causing her to conclude—'Oh, how jarring anything like the sound of merriment is to deep affliction.' Others however must have rejoiced to see the new Marquis no longer merit the reputation of being an enigmatic recluse indifferent to the customs among his own kind.

Lady Lansdowne was equally energetic in making that empty, curiously contrived building in Southampton a lively home for her husband and daughters. When Lansdowne decided that the great house at Bowood should have its doors locked, its windows made blind with shutters, and be left silently to brood on the past until his successor inherited the problem of deciding its fate, his wife saw to it that the choicest furniture went to furnish the Castle. And with it came portraits of Robespierre, Buonaparte, Marat and Curran and a sculptured head of Massena, and much else to transform bare compartments and corridors into elegant chambers and galleries.

The lack of 'grounds' about the Castle where stabling and coach-houses appropriate to the residence could be located posed a problem, as did also

**Lansdowne Castle, from the west, circa 1807.**

Artist and engraver unknown

the narrowness of the main approach, Castle Lane. It was solved, according to an eye-witness, Jane Austen's nephew, when staying with his grandmother and his aunt, the tenants of the house we have mentioned, seaward from the Castle, in an ingenious elegant and gaze-provoking way. He wrote that 'The Marchioness had a light phaeton drawn by six and sometimes eight, little ponies, each pair decreasing in size, and becoming lighter in colour, through all the grades of dark brown, light brown, bay and chestnut, as it was placed further away from the carriage. The two leading pairs were managed by two boyish postillions, the two pairs nearest the carriage were driven in hand. It was a delight to me to look down from the window and see this fairy equipage put together; for the premises of this Castle were so contracted that the whole process went on in the little space that remained of the open square.'

The Lansdownes took some part in the provincial jollity of the town, notably when they gave 'a grand fête', presumably in Castle Square, on the occasion of the Southampton Races in August, 1807.

There was one pastime of her husband's to which Lady Lansdowne took exception but which he would not give up, probably on the excuse that it was good for his health—sailing. After *Frisk* had gone to war her owner acquired a small yacht for day-sailing and when he moved from Peartree Green to Castle Square the yacht changed her moorings from off the ferry landing below the Green to the boat-yard near the West Quay. Lady Lansdowne's apprehension was seen to be justified one day when the Marquis was sailing in the Test opposite his home, when the yacht capsized and he and his crew were thrown into the water. By fortunate chance the Margravine of Anspach saw the catastrophe, ran to the boat-yard and initiated rescue by boat. She then hastened up to the Castle and warned her friend to have her husband's bed warmed and hot soup prepared ready for the return of her man, chilled and dripping after his adventure. When he had recovered he may have conceded that another such capsize would not be good for his health. While prepared to give up sailing in an open boat he would not give up sailing. He decided to acquire a larger, decked cutter more comparable with *Frisk*.

The first clue regarding where and when the new vessel was to be built came in a letter written by Jane Austen to her sister Cassandra, but in following up that clue it became apparent that her remarks on the Lansdownes' private affairs should not be relied upon for accuracy. Although the Austens were such close neighbours their relationship was that of polite acquaintances rather than that of friends. Jane wrote on 1st October, 1808,—'The Marquis put off being cured for another year; after waiting some weeks in vain for the return of the vessel he had agreed for, he is gone into Cornwall to order a vessel built for himself by a famous man in that country, on which he means to go abroad a twelvemonth hence.' Although the Customs House registers for that period in Cornwall were, like those for Southampton already mentioned, destroyed by fire in 1814, shipping intelligence for the port of Fowey in the local press, coupled with a study of Cornish shipbuilders, offer no alternative to the following conclusion. Lansdowne must have ordered his new yacht in the Spring of 1808, almost certainly not later than June, from Thomas Shepherd of Mevagissey, a builder of the highest reputation which led to a prolific number of launchings from his yard between 1785 and 1810. The only vessel described as a 'yacht', all others being one of the commercial descriptions, either arriving at or sailing from Fowey, in which Mevagissey was included, was the *Henry,* with a Captain Pearson as her master, which sailed for Southampton, 12th October 1808. Later newspapers reported that during the time of her voyage there were nor'westerly gales which drove ships ashore at Bideford, Ilfracombe and Barnstaple but the *Henry* would have been bowling along under the lee of the south coast where the strength of the gales would have been tempered by their passage across Devon and there would have been insufficient 'fetch' to build up a heavy sea. Lansdowne had not gone to Cornwall to order his yacht, some time in September, as Jane Austen thought, but to take delivery of it. It is scarcely conceivable that her enthusiastic owner, a man now of great experience in sailing such a vessel and longing to go to sea again since he parted with *Frisk,* did not sail with Pearson for Southampton. It must have been an exhilerating and speedy passage.

Lansdowne's choice of *Henry* as the name for his new yacht seems most likely to have been a gesture to his half-brother and heir-presumptive who at that time had angrily accused him of denuding Bowood of its timber for immediate financial gain and without thought for the reasonable expectations of a successor to the estate. If it was, then it did not succeed in stopping Henry from seeking restraint through the Courts, as a front-page report in the *Hampshire Chronicle,* dated 20th November 1809, shows. 'The Court of Chancery having some time since issued an injunction prohibiting the Marquis of Lansdowne from cutting down trees on his estate at Bowood, on the plea that the interest of the heirs in remainder were inquired, Sir A. Piggot on Tuesday applied, on behalf of the Marquis, for the removal of this injunction. He produced a variety of affidavits from the Surveyors of Woodlands, the object of which was to shew, that though the Marquis in the space of four years had cut down to the value of more than £40,000, yet so extensive were the plantations that this had only thinned them, and was necessary for the growth of the younger trees. It was also contended that the ornamental parts of those woods in the park surrounding the Mansion had received no deterioration and that nothing had been cut down which could be considered as ornamental to the grounds. Mr Alexander at length on the same side, and the further hearing was postponed.' Counsel did not however report to his client the way things had gone and his hopes for the outcome of the next hearing, because that evening, at Lansdowne House, John Henry Petty, marquis of Lansdowne, died.

*The Times* could not have said less or put the news into a less important place. In a column of snippets, following each other without headlines, below 'According to the latest advices Lord Wellesley's suite and baggage had been embarked at Cadiz in the *Donegal*', and above 'Mr Canning has taken apartments in the Albany. His furniture was removed thither from his house in Bruton Street on Tueday', there was simply 'The Marquis of Lansdowne died on Tuesday. His Lordship leaving no issue, is succeeded in his title and estate by his brother Lord Henry Petty.' It did not publish an obituary but described the funeral procession, which included four Earls, an Irish Archbishop and, contrary to custom, a lady, all close friends of the late Marquis, a relative of his widow but none of his own, together with his executors and principal servants. Unlike itself, *The Gentleman's Magazine* could do no better than copy *The Times'* description of the funeral and embellish the prose more to its style. The only obituary from an informed source appeared in the *Hampshire Chronicle* of November 27th, recalling first John Henry Petty's unusual upbringing as already related. It then draws from causes and effects experienced in his youth to explain his behaviour towards some of his fellow men in later years. The author was almost certainly James Linden, sometime editor and publisher of the *Hampshire Chronicle* and, after he had sold the paper to a Winchester printer, its principal correspondent for the Southampton locality. As the proprietor of Linden's Library he had gained a reputation as a minor writer and scholar. The content of this obituary betrays a closer acquaintance with Lansdowne's life and philosophy than *The Times* ever had, both in the stated facts and in the following conclusion: 'Born with great good sense, an upright and benevolent heart, and equally disdaining hypocracy and disguise, his Lordship soon imbibed disgust at the machiavellian tricks and chicanery of trading diplomacy; from this cause and from his partial and imperfect early education, he was disposed to think worse of mankind in general, than he would have done had he been bred at a publick school, among noble and honorable equals, or had he invariably consulted his own excellent understanding. Having seen much of the intrigue of Foreign Courts, his mind, naturally elevated and noble, felt a kind of involuntary recoil. Though possessed of talents equal to the highest stations, he wished merely to be considered as a private gentleman; and they only could estimate his talents, his constructive conversation, and his powerful eloquence, who were among the number of his few and intimate friends, to whom he shewed a long, a sincere, and unvaried attachment.'

There remains in Southampton but one solid relic of the second Marquis of Lansdowne's residence there, a statue of George III standing in a nitch on the Bar Gate where a wooden figure of Queen Anne formerly mouldered. Lansdowne instructed the sculptor, as a special tribute to his Majesty, to depict him wearing the imperial dress and accoutrements as shown on the statue of the Emperor Hadrian in the British Museum. He did not see the sculpture finished and it had to be formally presented to the Town by his widow. Perhaps it would have been at least as appropriate if the king's opinion had been carved in stone somewhere at the same time—'The Marquis of Lansdowne is the best bred man I ever met with.'

The untimely death of the Marquis left his widow with the problem which had mainly determined her to leave Ireland—finishing the education of five daughters and, if not actually finding, at least creating the circumstances most likely to attract eligible young men to become their husbands. Remembering the malicious gossip which had been circulated in London society, this twice-widowed Welsh woman who was used to a happy Irish environment should be remembered not only for her bringing unusual happiness into the last few years of Lansdowne's life but also for the considerable success she achieved in the fierce, relentless battle for husbands fought in a hostile English field. She and the Miss Giffards continued to live in the Castle, content with the minor 'County' events, attendance at which contributed to their education, but when they attained a sufficiently mature age they returned to the strategically better placed Wycombe Lodge at Richmond. From there the eldest, Ann, married William Gerald Bagot, and the second girl, Harriet, married Henry Mellish. While we may assume that both these gentlemen were worthy and maybe well-connected, neither found their way into any of the registers, at least those based on wisdom, rank or acres, indicating public esteem. The next two, Eliza and Louisa, had not secured husbands up to the time of their mother's death but the youngest, Maria, startled society when she became a countess, by marrying a Florentine nobleman and diplomat, Count Lusi.

# 11

# A Corsican on Peartree Green

There was certainly a time when the suggestion that Napoleon had visited England would have made me preserve a respectful silence if it came from a stranger, or just grin in token of not taking the suggestion seriously of course but prepared to hear the rest of the joke, if it came from a friend. The diligent reader will recall however that CFC II made a tantalising remark suggesting that he had some knowledge of Napoleon which however he would not expect me to believe, at least until some corroborative evidence turned up, and how his son the Jesuit priest, when I asked about this after his father had died, told me that his father believed that Napoleon had been in England, in fact for at least some of the time at Peartree Green, and that his father's reticence had been due to his being ridiculed when, sometime, among some company, he announced this. As I understood it, none in his time could picture Napoleon as other than the greatest of great Frenchmen about whom revolved the destiny of Europe and whose outstanding military skill nearly destroyed Britain's liberty. What Cooksey believed was that a boy named Napoleone, a native of the rebellious island of Corsica, which had been sold by the Genoese to the French without the consent of the inhabitants, had visited Peartree Green. There would have been nothing remarkable about that if the grown-up boy had not reappeared later, on the world stage, as a Frenchman more Gallic than the Gauls but still identifiable as being once the Corsican boy. Had what I remembered of French history not been such a poor tribute to my masters, and had that little not been so biased by seeming to exist only where the French rudely interrupted the familiar flow of British history, then I might have been less tardy in tackling this question. And it must be admitted that its pursuit was due more to curiosity than any conviction that Cooksey would be found to have been right. What follows, therefore, should be looked upon as bringing the story up-to-date rather than to its ending.

It was daunting to learn at the beginning of my inquiries that a German library had, some years ago, catalogued over 200,000 different works under the general subject-heading *Napoleon,* and the number must have been increasing ever since. On further inquiry it appeared that diligent scholars had shown that many of those works were more fictitious than true, written by authors bent on making money from a very large but injudicious readership avid for books about the great man now made more mysterious by being confined to a far distant island where from being a prisoner he became a martyr and finally a great national hero. Others, fearing for their future under the new regime, wrote accounts of events which, they hoped, would shed a more favourable light on their behaviour and explain away anything which otherwise might be looked upon with distaste beyond the tolerance of their new masters. Modern scholars, I found, regarded Frêderic Masson as *the* authority on the life of Napoleon. It is upon his *Notes sur la jeunesse de Napoléon (1769-1793)* that reliance is mainly placed. The British Library also produced two other books with significant although short passages originating from English boys who were at Brienne with Napoleone, Sir William Fraser's *Hic et Ubique* (Sampson Low 1893) and, by an author hiding behind the initials 'C.H.', *Some account of the early years of Buonaparte at the Military School of Brienne* (London 1797). The boy in the firstnamed book was Lawley, son of a baronet and who later became Lord Wenlock, of a peerage which became extinct not many years back. Only boys 'of family' were accepted at Brienne.

Extracts from these and from other works more easily available had to lay in my desk undisturbed, *force majeure,* for a vexatiously long time. Had I known during that time that a distinguished historian, Mr Vincent Cronin, was going over the same ground, and very much more, gathering material for his *Napoleon* (Collins, 1971), I would have suffered fewer pangs of conscience every time I happened to see those languishing papers. Mr Cronin, I was happy to find, cited the same books from which extracts were in my desk. He did not know the Cooksey story until after his book was published but had in fact pursued from evidence he had the possibility that Napoleone, the Corsican schoolboy, came to England. In reply to my letter, telling him of the Cooksey story, Mr Cronin convinced me that his strenuous search in the Public Record Office and at Greenwich for certain missing papers left nothing for me to try excepting possibly archives or private collections containing letters written by the English schoolboy Lawley, or the other, C.H., from Brienne, or in biographical notes written in later life. The result of this search, albeit for papers whose continued existence was only a hopeful possibility, was disappointing, but not to the degree that Mr Cronin must have suffered since he was looking for papers which, but for some accident, or more likely an acquisitive thief, ought to have been carefully preserved where he looked.

I had suggested that a possible motive for Napoleone's visit was to acquire first-hand knowledge of the Naval Acadmey at Portsmouth, or even to approach one of the staff which, at that time, was not very formidable, consisting of a Governor, a First Master, an Usher, a French Master, a Drawing Master and a Surgeon. This drew from Mr Cronin the only possibly adverse comment on what I had told him. 'I do not think', he wrote, 'he would have spend his scant pay merely on a reconnaisance of the Naval Academy,' a point to be considered later.

In order to understand the character of Napoleone when he was at school in Brienne, as a pointer to what he is likely to have done under certain circumstances, we must go back to his parents and his childhood in Corsica, an island whose political history is too convoluted for more than the briefest mention here. The Corsicans were continually in revolt against their rulers, first the Genoese, then the French, a brief spell under the British and finally back to the French under whom the yearning for freedom from foreign rule is still not extinguished. The outstanding leader of the rebel forces was Paoli who, after remarkable successes in attacking French troops from bases within the natural security of wild, mountainous country, was finally outwitted and had to surrender, albeit on generous terms. Carlo Buona Parte, a lawyer descended from a noble Italian family, had been with Paoli as his secretary and assistant, and had represented Paoli's case to the Pope and to the government in Paris. When there was some fear that the French would hold him and his family hostage, Carlo and his wife, Letisia, and their son Giuseppe, saddled-up and took to the hills, finally arriving at Paoli's headquarters in a remote cave. Negotiating the rocky, almost trackless terrain, the horses having to be led on foot as often as they could be ridden, was not without considerable apprehension for Letisia, who had lost her first and second-born children, for she was carrying her fourth child, destined to be named after an uncle, Napoleone.

Louis XV's instructions to his representative in Corsica, the Comte de Vaux, were to induce the Corsicans to behave as good citizens of France, which in law they were if not in heart, but to do this gently, and generously if need be. Consequently Paoli was allowed to take the British offer to accept him in England as an exile and to give him a passage in a British warship. His aide-de-camp had the choice of going into exile with Paoli or of serving the Comte de Vaux, who needed such educated, French-speaking Corsicans as could be gathered in to help with the new administration. It was a balancing point in history; had the Bona Parte family gone to England with Paoli then Napoleone would have been born British, learned English and perhaps become one of the forty young gentlemen being educated at the Royal Naval Academy in Portsmouth and still learn as a foreign language, French. We need speculate no further as to his chances of becoming a great admiral because of course there would have been no Napoleon on the other side.

Carlo's decision to accept the situation with the prospect of a head start in the new provincial government and a good, regular salary eventually brought him valuable favour from the new governor, M. de Marbeuf. Marbeuf persuaded the ministry in Paris that, as part of the package deal to pacify the Corsicans, Carlo Buona Parte's nobility should be recognised officially, so entitling one of his sons a place in a State Military School. Giuseppe was destined for the Church, so Napoleone was given a place in the school at Brienne, but as he knew no French, Napoleone was taken to Autun, roughly a French equivalent to Eton, with his elder brother, aged then 9 and 11, for an intensive course in French in preparation for entering Brienne and a seminary at Aix respectively, four months later. They were received at Autun by Marbeuf's nephew, the Bishop of Autun who, like Marbeuf, was not constricted by lack of means and was generous to the boys.

Certain linguistic peculiarities accompanied Napoleone to Brienne, such as using the Italian form of some common French words and, when excited, lapsing into Italian pronunciation, which resulted in his being marked down from the beginning for mocking imitation of his worst faults in French by the less kindly of the other boys. This treatment only increased his natural aversion for his schoolfellows, excepting perhaps the English, who represented to him those who had unjustly fought his father, killed his uncle and banished his parents' great friend Paoli, as he had learned at school in Corsica and from his parents and Giuseppe. His becoming a loner served to develop in him an independent outlook, to intensify his ability to study and, unwittingly, to ensure a sympathetic response from his masters whenever the need might arise.

All pupils at Brienne, or at the other eleven Royal Military Schools, other than foreign students, aspired to become officers in either the army or the navy. There were some differences in the curriculum between that of a would-be soldier and that of another looking to becoming an admiral. In particular the latter concentrated on mathematics. In the dormitories the military 'men' slept on wooden beds; the naval 'men' slept in hammocks. When Napoleone's mother visited the school, and Napoleone's stocks went up because of Letisia's great charm and beauty, she was horrified when she learned why her boy slept in a hammock instead of a bed as all civilised boys should. To contemplate the possibility of her son someday having to fight in a battle at sea, which involved enduring the perils of the deep all the time, was incomprehensible. However, she was unable to get Napoleone to change his mind.

In 1783 the Treaty of Versailles put an official end to a war between Britain and France which in effect had ended some months earlier, which explains why the English boys could have been at Brienne during that year. It also accounts for Napoleone's plans to enter the French navy being upset, for most of its ships were being laid up and their officers put on half-pay or retired. Bearing in mind that Napoleone at that time considered that he had no obligation to France, and that Britain had shown sympathy for the Corsicans when it took Paoli to England at the time of his defeat, he would have seen a way out of his dilemma in seeking a place at the Royal Naval Academy at Portsmouth. The evidence for his having made the attempt comes from Fraser, as follows:

> 'One day the little Corsican came to young Lawley, and said "Look at this": he showed him a letter written in remarkably good English: it was addressed to the British Admiralty; and requested permission to enter our Navy. The young Buonaparte said "The difficulty I am afraid will be my religion." Lawley said "You young rascal; I don't believe that you have any religion at all." Napoleone replied "But my family have: my mother's race, the Ramolini, are very rigid: I should be disinherited if I showed any signs of becoming a heretic." These facts I had from one who had very good means of knowing: he told me that Buonaparte's letter was sent: and that it still exists in the archives of the Admiralty. I have not searched for it; for the simple reason that I do not wish so good a story to become prematurely public. I hope that someone who has access to the historical documents in that department may take the trouble to find it."

It was Mr Cronin who went to the trouble to try to find that letter, and he personally assured me that he took no end of trouble. In his book he states 'The collection of letters in which N's application would be is not in the P.R.O. and seems to have disappeared, together with the Admiralty in-letter book for that period. However, the Notebooks of Alexandre des Mazis provide new evidence of N's determination to go to sea; and the incident is quite in character with what we know of the young N.'

There can be no doubt that Napoleone, while at school in Brienne and throughout his time at the *École Militaire,* and for some time beyond, was openly a Corsican patriot whose ever present desire was to see his country liberated from French or any other foreign rule. This obsession was well known among his companions, as is shown by a prank they played on him. The young gentlemen at Brienne were required to wear their hair in a queue tied with a distinguishing ribbon which was a specific part of their uniform. One of the French boys stealthily attached to the end of Napoleone's ribbon a figure described in Masson as 'un petit Paoli' designed to promote sniggering while the victim was still puzzled as to the cause and, on its being discovered, an explosion of anger. A further indication was given by the English boy 'C.H.' who criticised Napoleone on moral grounds for saying that he would someday fight to free Corsica from the French while at the same time he accepted from the French free education at Brienne.

The desire to go to sea, in the British navy if the French navy could not fulfil his hopes, was not his only motive and maybe not his principal motive, for trying to get to the academy in Portsmouth. The course at the Military College lasted four years after which successful pupils went on immediately to the *École Militaire.* Carlo had reckoned that Napoleone, who had entered the school in 1779, would leave in 1783 and that Napoleone's younger brother Lucien would be given a place in the school under the same government bursary. In the examinations in 1783 Napoleone did well, especially in mathematics; in history and geography he was good and only in dancing and drawing he 'could have done better'. He was academically qualified for the next step but the inspecting officer, the Chevalier de Kéralio, considered that he was not yet old enough to be thrown with older boys into the rigid routine at the *École* in Paris. He was assigned a place in the next year's instake, when Napoleone would be fifteen. It was not until the next day that the Bishop of Autun arrived to see Napoleone and the Father Superior, too late to influence Kéralio's decision, and it was most likely with his tacit agreement, and with perhaps something more substantial that Napoleone went to his friendly English master for sympathy, advice and co-operation, for the necessary letter to the Admiralty must not betray that his English was less than adequate. The 'remarkably good English' noted by Lawley one feels must have been achieved through the kind heart and sage understanding of the lay brother charged with teaching English to the budding sailors in the school, (the budding soldiers were taught German), who was helped perhaps by a wistful hope that he too might see England soon.

In such a delicate matter as letting a boy go on an extra-curricular journey into a foreign country on his own initiative, and perhaps in this case miscounting the numbers on the school roll so that for a time the presence of Napoleone and Lucien together would pass unnoticed, there would be nothing on record which might cause some busybody from the Ministry to require an explanation. Surely there could be nothing wrong in encouraging a boy to improve his English by taking a holiday in England at his own expense. Napoleone must have had a considerable nest-egg by his fourth year at Brienne, accumulated from de Marbeuf's regular remittances to enable Napoleone to pay for his needs on the same scale as the other boys, most if not all of whom were the sons of wealthy parents, were accustomed to spend. But his needs had been very modest; he had only once gone on a considerable journey, to Brittany to visit some distant relatives, and at school the only extraordinary but probably small expense was for the materials to put up a little fence round his garden plot, the cultivation of which he took most seriously. The 'owners' of the adjoining plots had little respect for Napoleone's seed-beds or tender plants if crossing his plot was the shortest way to wherever they were going. The generous Bishop would have left the whole business in the capable care of the two Fathers who were the joint heads of the school. That care would put the accumulation of funds to meet some unforseen contingency, such as had occurred in 1783, before the ephemeral pleasures on which pocket-money usually melted away.

So long as the young traveller was content with using the economical water-buses and was happy to pace the miles along the cross-country paths connecting the key points on the rivers and canals where another water-bus could be boarded, taking simple sustenance on the way and modest accommodation at night, the cost of the journey overland from Brienne to Havre de Grace would not be great. There he would have found that the advertised adult fare on the Southampton packet was, for those who carried guineas in their purse, one and a half guineas, and for others the equivalent in louis and francs, a sum making that day's expenditure more than on any other but not so much that Napoleone would have considered it too high a price to pay in the pursuit of his urgent and important purpose.

The term ended at Brienne on 14th September 1783 and, assuming that Napoleone in his eagerness would have wasted no time starting or on the way and assuming of course that our lead up to where the Cooksey history begins is reasonable, the Corsican would have become the guest of the packet's Captain, James Bryer, and his family on Peartree Green before that month was out. To link this with the Peartree end of the story, as it was related by Father Fred Cooksey when we sat alone in the garden-studio in Southampton, there had to be a girl in the family of an age at which the writing of letters would be an ordinary accomplishment, and there also needed to be others old enough and living close enough to have met and talked with the visitor sufficiently to keep him and the circumstances impressed on their memories enough to be able to recall them about thirty years later, when there began to appear biographies of Napoleon, from one of which the Bryers could have read of his Corsican origin and of his being at school in Brienne. Before the defeat of Napoleon in 1815 any biography of him in Linden's Library or in the magazines would have been more a commentary on a very present and formidable enemy of Britain about whom the only question was how could he be vanquished. There would be no good purpose at that stage to inquire into his infancy and schooling even if a British writer had facts which French writers did not find until after 1815. The brief account by 'C.H.', printed but probably not widely published in 1797, was an exception and of limited content which, however, if it were read on Peartree Green, would have awakened the memories of an older generation than that to which the following is confined.

Ruling out all Bryer girls then living on Peartree Green who were younger than Napoleone, there remains only James Bryer's daughter Elizabeth to be the letter-writer and had need to make a note of Napoleone's address at Brienne. She was of the same age and although so far the end of her life is not written into the family tree it contains evidence that she lived well into the next century. Others of around Napoleone's age also there at the time who would have remembered him after 1815 were Elizabeth's brother Thomas, the master-mariner who turned parson, and her cousin William, the privateer, both of whom John Cooksey numbered among his friends as well as close relatives by marriage. James, Napoleone's host, and his brother John both lived a few years beyond that of Waterloo and could have drawn upon their memories but their sisters Elizabeth and Mary, much longer lived, may have talked about it at the time of the Christening of George Napoleon Cooksey, the first of the commemorative succession. His mother was scarcely two when we may presume Napoleone patted her on the head but with a father and mother, an aunt and an uncle, a sister and two brothers, a first cousin and no doubt others who could speak from first-hand knowledge she must have been fully convinced that Napoleon as a second name for little George was justified by historical fact.

Napoleone's poor command of English would not have made any difficulty in the Bryer household. As in all Southampton families concerned in commerce with France, French was one of the essentials. After the children were grounded in grammar and vocabulary at any of the 'academies' in the town they went, often at quite an early age, following the axiom 'never too young to teach their tongue', to an establishment in France to improve pronunciation and acquire fluency. One such establishment was opened in Calais by an enterprising Southampton woman who had a number of the Bryer clan among her pupils. The last of these came home early to tell of how, after seeing some friends off in the English packet one Sunday evening, he strolled back to the school but was horrified to find that during his absence it had become a smouldering ruin. One reason for sending the children to France was to avoid the dire results of their listening to the hybrid tongue spoken in the so-called French quarter of Southampton, between St Michael's Church and the Town Quay.

Although the colony sprang from Huguenots the founders had come not from France but from the Low Countries.

Alas, George Napoleon Cooksey died without issue but when his next born nephew was Christened he was given the single name Napoleon. This second Napoleon Cooksey begat daughters but no son. The succession again took a sidestep to the grandson of another of George Napoleon's brothers, who was named Walter Bertrand Napoleon Cooksey. He was a celibate priest and had neither nephew nor a male first cousin and with him the line commemorating the Corsican boy became extinct.

As to the story in *The Tablet,* a look-out was kept for any information which might fit it, especially among the records of Napoleone's time at the *École Militaire* in Paris and in the short space before he returned to Corsica on leave. It is not impossible that he was introduced to a young lady from Winchester when she was visiting Paris nor for a determined cadet or subaltern to make a hasty visit to Winchester via Southampton during say a fortnight's or three weeks' leave, but no evidence came to light.

# 12

# One Last Look from Peartree Green

For William Bryer, sometime yacht-master to the Earl of Wycombe, sometime privateer, the years of peace which followed Waterloo were marred, first by the death of his wife, then that of his father who was followed within a year by his uncle James, the two men to whom he owed all he had learned of the sea and much of what he knew of life ashore since his life and theirs had been closely and happily intertwined for as long as he could remember. Except for his son William, the schoolmaster and navigator, he was the last of the Bryers of Peartree Green. He resolved to leave his sorrows on the Green, marry Sarah Petty from a Southampton family he had long known, and resettle in pastures new, at Warsash, just across the river from the cottage on the quay at Hamble where his son came, as regular as a chronometer, to teach navigation.

His going to Warsash did not separate father and son; in fact it resulted in more frequent contact, and at predictable times, than they had become accustomed to make when living only half a mile apart in their native parish. True, their new contacts were often no more than a wave of the hand across the river signifying 'all's well and nothing urgent to report'. At other times father would cross the river and take bread and cheese with his son between the morning and afternoon sessions in the school, when news from the land north of the Hamble would be exchanged for that from the south. There was an intermediate method of communication when either noticed something of interest to the other in their respective newspapers. The item would be marked and perhaps something written in the margin, and the paper given to the ferry-man to deliver across the river. Just such a despatch crossed from north to south during the first year of exodus, 1818. The paper reported that the Comte de Flahault, Buonaparte's aide-de-camp at Waterloo, had eloped with the daughter of Lord Keith, the admiral who had watched for Buonaparte's ships putting to sea, year in, year out, in all weathers, in cramped quarters and on a restricted diet until his health was quite ruined. Any Frenchman, and especially one who had been so closely connected with his arch enemy as was Flahault, was anathema to him. When this French count, who spoke English better than many of the admiral's English circle, asked for the hand of his daughter in marriage Flahault was dismissed with that promptness, that clarity and with that emphasis which can be attained only by long service in the Navy in command of some of the most unpromising crews the press-gangs could assemble. The calm which returned to the Keith household after that short but violent storm was suddenly shattered when the admiral's look-outs reported that that audacious Frenchman and his daughter had left, presumably headed for Gretna Green, two days earlier. Keith could only order an immediate chase by the best riders and swiftest horses available to him; he himself was no longer fit for such strenuous business and had to endure, as he had often done before, inactive days and sleepless nights waiting for news. When the vexing, irreversible truth was brought to him in Devon he realised that he had been beaten by the exercise of that age-old stratagem—surprise. The runaways had turned off the road which led to the nearest point on the border where one could leave the jurisdiction of England and turn to ones purpose the more accommodating laws of Scotland, Gretna Green, and headed for Edinburgh. There, not over an anvil but in St Andrew's Church in fashionable George Street, Charles Comte de Flahault and Margaret Mercer Elphinstone, daughter of Admiral Viscount Keith, were married with ceremony befitting their station and among many of their friends. Young William had written in the margin of the newspaper 'This must be the boy great-uncle told me he brought from Havre after your Lord Wycombe smuggled him out of Paris during the Revolution.'

In 1824, after six uneventful years with Sarah at Warsash, with no desire to re-visit Peartree Green, William senior was induced to change his mind by his hearing, over bread, cheese and ale, a description of the astonishing box-like, steam-driven contraption which, his son said, could carry coach and horses across the Itchen, as well as more passengers than would fill five ferry boats. How could a ship, or whatever it was called, however it was driven through the water, be steered without a rudder? It had no seamen, only an engineer and a stoker and a man to scotch the wheels of the coaches; that couldn't be right. When he was told that it was all done by chains his bewilderment was complete and he agreed to hire a cob at Hamble and accompany his son to the schoolhouse, to stay a few days and to see it all for himself.

A messenger having been sent overnight to John Cooksey in the High Street and to cousin Josiah at the Bell Inn down the lane opposite, the dwindling clansmen gathered at the latest replacement of the old elm

**The new steam-driven 'Floating Bridge' at the Southampton side.**

From a drawing by T. Nash, circa 1836

bench on the crest of the Green. There below them was what the local newspaper chose to call the 'floating bridge', behaving like a beetle uncertain of where it wanted to go, wobbling in a cross-tide between two chains which could be seen lying on the beach side by side and anchored above high-water mark, a little downstream from the Royal Oak on one side and the Cross House on the other. And that was not all that affronted the gaze of the returned native. From God's House Tower nearly to the Cross House the leafy avenue along the Beach, as it was misleadingly called, if the trees were not felled, was hidden by new quays which at one point formed a basin which was packed with ships, their swinging derricks loading directly into open wagons or piling bales and baulks on the quayside.

It was not only the evidence of his eyes which dispelled the perfection of the scene as long remembered; his nose detected a foreign, sulphurous smell in the air. Down on the water there were new vessels, cross-channel packets, tug-boats and even the 'floating-bridge', streaming smoke onto the wind, not the lazy, faintly blue, whisps of wood smoke that rose from homely hearths but black, expanding billows which climbed on the sou'west breeze up the hill and over the Green.

Someone pointed out that Lansdowne Castle no longer overtopped the town, to which John Cooksey contributed news of the latest development in Castle Square. First, the castle mound had been levelled, leaving not a trace of the Castle or its outbuildings. The first new building in the Square was to be a dissenters' chapel to the cost of which William Chamberlayne, whose house they could see across the common and who was one of the town's MPs, had subscribed thirty pounds although he was of the Church established. Not to be outdone in the new age of tolerance, the Jews of the town were planning to build themselves a synagogue on the other side of the Square. The Marquis wouldn't have approved that, interposed Josiah Bryer; he was a very strict Churchman. He gave special instructions in his Will where he was to be buried according to where he died. If he had died in his Castle he was to be taken to Rumsey Abbey and buried next to his ancestor Sir William Petty.

During the lifetime of the late Marquis, and indeed since, the elder William would rarely talk about his Lordship's affairs, but after a decent interval of fifteen years, and since cousin Josiah had mentioned Sir William Petty, he told a story which he had discovered through his wife, Sarah Petty. Lord Wycombe had once taken him to Rumsey in a curricle, without a groom, it being convenient that way to talk over his plans for his next voyage in *Frisk*. After the horses had been put up and his Lordship was setting off about his own business, he suggested that he should have a look at the Abbey and at his ancestor's tomb in the graveyard. At the

Abbey door he asked a gentleman if he could direct him to that part of the graveyard where he should look for Sir William Petty's tomb. On learning why he was interested, the gentleman very kindly showed him Sir William's tomb and afterwards took him to see what remained of the house where his parents lived, next to their cloth-mill, talking all the time about Sir William's remarkable life, including the fact which his Lordship had once mentioned, during one of the voyages to Ireland, that Sir William had been a sailor, both before the mast and on the poop, and therefore his Lordship had salt-water in his veins which would ensure his becoming a good sailor. But this gentleman at Rumsey told him much more from which he could well understand why his Lordship held Sir William in such high esteem. His parents were humble folk from families in the cloth-making trade established round Basingstoke. They moved down to Rumsey and set up a cloth-mill of their own. Their son was given the best schooling they could afford but could make no better start in life than going to sea. He did not get on well with his fo'castle mates, because he was a scholar and seemed to belong to the officer class, and when he broke a leg onboard he was put ashore in France and abandoned to his own contrivings if he survived the devoted but crude nursing skills of the nuns in a local hospice. He recovered and immediately turned to earning money to repay the hospice by teaching English and Navigation. That done he saved his earnings until he had enough to enter the Jesuit College in Caen to perfect his French. He then returned to England and entered the Navy as a navigator and French interpreter. On the outbreak of the Civil War he decided that it would be imprudent to be associated with either faction, resigned from the Navy and returned to the Continent, where he studied at four unviersities until the war came to an end. Back again in England he busied himself at Rumsey making improvements to the old mill-machinery. And remembering his sailoring he then invented an unsinkable ship, which was built and worked regularly across the Irish sea. That wasn't all: he was made a professor at Oxford and finished up making the first proper map of Ireland. He thought that some of his Lordship's business when they had gone to Ireland was about some land which belonged to Sir William. But the point of the Captain's story, to which Sir William Petty's biography was a necessary lead, was that his wife had told him that her grandfather Petty and his father were in the cloth business at Basingstoke.

Did his Lordship ever talk about his family, asked one of the circle, other than he should see his ancestor's tomb at Rumsey Abbey? No, not really, excepting once when they were anchored in Dublin Bay and two of his friends, as Irish as they make'em, rowed out and came onboard. It was a warm evening with a nice little breeze, so they sat on the steering-bench talking. Presently his Lordship called to his man to fetch wine and four glasses, and then invited him, as he often did on such occasions, to join them. They were talking about the state of things in Kerry, away in the sou'west, causing his Lordship to say that it hadn't changed there much since his forebear, Tom FitzMaurice, was made Baron of Kerry five-hundred, yes, five-hundred years before. Whether that was his quiet way of showing these Irish gentlemen that he had some pretty deep roots in their country he wasn't sure but he went on to tell about the tough life those early barons lived. One of them, he said, was so worn out with riding out every day to settle a quarrel, investigate a murder or chase off a band of cattle-stealers that he decided to hand over to his son and to end his days quietly in a monastery. Life was so different as a lay brother in the monastery that he lived to see his son wear himself out and die and his second son take over, and lived on a few years after that. Another story he told was about another of his ancestors who took a neighbour to court to have a dispute, about which of them rightly owned a stretch of land, settled by the judge. Of course this Baron Kerry wouldn't have taken the other to court if he wasn't sure in himself that he would win, but the judge gave it to the other man, name of MacCarthy he thought, on which the Baron sprang at MacCarthy and killed him right there in front of the judge.

After such recollections, when almost unrelated pickings of history were passed on to a younger generation, conversation turned to current affairs. Yes, said John Cooksey, Sir William Champion de Crespigny still had Anspach House but he was often away in Wales, where he had another house, and of course in London, but he had suggested that he would not stand for Parliament again now that he was getting on in years. Little George Napoleon had just had his first birthday; no, he didn't seem to mind being called Napoleon. Josiah's choice of news was the seizure in the river a week back, from an Itchen Ferry fishing smack, of 51 tubs of contraband spirits. Those who wonderd how Josiah had become the owner of The Bell at a comparatively early age were inclined to think that his expert knowledge of smuggling practice held the clue but of course never revealed their thoughts. Then there was the fishing, a parallel industry but not so lucrative; so many herrings had been netted in the river only a few days back that, according to the new *Southampton Herald,* none of them fetched more than a ha'penny a dozen in the market and most of them were dumped on the fields at Northam as manure. Not such luck as they had had in 1823 when a shoal was trapped in the river above the ferry and they took a thousand—nine-hundred, corrected Cooksey—nine-hundred bushels during the night. And next morning when the Frenchies came in, they sold the lot over the gunnels at four shillings a bushel. It was a good bargain for both sides.

The visit over, with parting invitations to his friends to sail down to Warsash next time, where Sarah would welcome them too, the two Williams rode next day side-by-side down to Hamble, one thinking that the visit had been a great success, the other resolved never to go back, whatever crazy thing they might think of next to spoil Peartree Green.

'Young' William achieved more years than any other Bryer of his time, over three score and ten. For twenty years after his father's last visit to the Green he regularly jogged between his two schools, carrying his panniers of books and mail and then sold the school at Peartree, to settle finally in Hamble. In 1921, the late Gregory Robinson, the marine painter, acquired a cottage-studio in which to develop sketches he had made on a sailing ship during a voyage 'round the Horn' and made inquiries about it among the older inhabitants in the village. One couple remembered 'Billy' Bryer from their youth, and with great affection. Gregory Robinson had bought Billy's navigation school, almost unaltered, the last cottage on the quay at Hamble.

It must have been in 1843 that Billy Bryer would have read in his paper that Lord Henry Petty-FitzMaurice, heir apparent of the Marquis of Lansdowne, had married Emily Jane Mercer Elphinstone de Flahault. Was his natural impulse to outline the item and write something in the margin, such as 'The wheel has turned full circle'? Then beginning to nod off, the newspaper slipping unheeded to the floor, he might just have remembered that the name of the ferry-man on the river was not Charon,. . . it was Jurd, Harry Jurd. . . there was no need to trouble him with any paper now.